Machine Learning with Kubernetes

A Hands-On Guide to Building, Deploying, and Managing Intelligent Applications

Martin Dunagan

Copyright © 2024 Martin Dunagan

All rights reserved. No part of this book may be reproduced, stored in a retrieval system, or transmitted, in any form or by any means, electronic, mechanical, photocopying, recording, or otherwise, without the prior written permission of the author, except in the case of brief quotations embodied in critical reviews and certain other noncommercial uses permitted by copyright law.

Disclaimer

This book is for educational and informational purposes only. It is not intended as financial, legal, or investment advice. The author and publisher do not guarantee accuracy, completeness, or timeliness of the information and are not responsible for errors or omissions.

Cryptocurrency and blockchain investments are highly speculative and involve significant risk. The author and publisher are not liable for any losses or damages incurred.

The views expressed are those of the author and do not reflect the publisher's views. Specific product or company mentions do not constitute endorsements.

Readers should conduct their own research and consult qualified professionals before making financial or investment decisions related to blockchain technology or cryptocurrencies

Table of Contents

Preface..7
Chapter 1: Introduction..9
    1.1 Convergence of Machine Learning and Kubernetes.................9
    1.2 Why Kubernetes for Machine Learning?....................................15
    1.3 Machine Learning Workflow Overview.......................................19
    1.4 Kubernetes Fundamentals...23
    1.5 Book Structure and Conventions...28
Chapter 2: Setting Up Your Kubernetes Environment....................33
    2.1 Choosing a Kubernetes Distribution..33
    2.2 Installing and Configuring kubectl..37
    2.3 Understanding Kubernetes Concepts...42
    2.4 Working with Kubernetes Resources..46
    2.5 Troubleshooting and Debugging..52
Chapter 3: Containerizing Machine Learning Applications..............57
    3.1 Introduction to Docker and Containerization..............................57
    3.2 Building Docker Images for Machine Learning.........................60
    3.3 Packaging ML Models and Dependencies................................64
    3.4 Optimizing Docker Images for Size and Performance..............69
    3.5 Security Considerations for Containerized ML Applications.....73
Chapter 4: Building Machine Learning Workflows..........................77
    4.1 Orchestrating Data Pipelines..77
    4.2 Running Distributed Training Jobs..83
    4.3 Hyperparameter Tuning and Model Selection...........................88
    4.4 Managing Data and Model Versioning..91
Chapter 5: Deploying Machine Learning Models............................96
    5.1 Deployment Patterns..96
    5.2 Exposing Models with Kubernetes Services and Ingress.........102
    5.3 A/B Testing and Canary Deployments for ML............................106
    5.4 Monitoring Model Performance and Health...............................112
Chapter 6: Scaling and Resource Management............................116
    6.1 Understanding Resource Requests and Limits.........................116
    6.2 Auto Scaling Machine Learning Applications............................120

6.3 Optimizing Resource Allocation for Cost Efficiency................. 124
  6.4 GPU Management and Acceleration... 127
Chapter 7: Managing Machine Learning Pipelines......................**132**
  7.1 CI/CD for Machine Learning Workflows..................................132
  7.2 Experiment Tracking and Artifact Management....................... 136
  7.3 Model Registry and Version Control.. 140
  7.4 Promoting Models to Production..144
Chapter 8: Security and Access Control... **148**
  8.1 Securing Your Kubernetes Cluster... 148
  8.2 Authentication and Authorization for ML Applications.............. 153
  8.3 Protecting Sensitive Data in Machine Learning....................... 157
  8.4 Security Best Practices for Kubernetes and ML...................... 161
Chapter 9: Advanced Topics and Future Trends........................... **165**
  9.1 Serverless Machine Learning with Knative.............................. 165
  9.2 Using GPUs and Hardware Accelerators................................. 169
  9.3 Federated Learning and Edge AI on Kubernetes..................... 173
  9.4 The Evolving Landscape of Cloud-Native ML..........................177
Conclusion... **180**

Preface

The world of software development is in constant flux, with new technologies and paradigms emerging at a breakneck pace. Among the most transformative advancements in recent years is the rise of cloud-native development, fueled by the power of containers and orchestration platforms like Kubernetes. At the same time, machine learning has exploded in popularity, revolutionizing industries and creating unprecedented opportunities for innovation. This book sits at the intersection of these two powerful trends, exploring how Kubernetes can be leveraged to build, deploy, and manage intelligent applications.

This book, "Machine Learning with Kubernetes: A Hands-On Guide to Building, Deploying, and Managing Intelligent Applications," is aimed at application developers, data scientists, and machine learning engineers who want to harness the capabilities of Kubernetes to streamline their ML workflows and unlock new possibilities. Whether you're just starting your journey with Kubernetes or looking to deepen your expertise, this book will provide you with the knowledge and practical skills needed to succeed.

Within these pages, you'll embark on a comprehensive exploration of using Kubernetes for machine learning. We'll begin with the fundamentals, laying a solid foundation in both machine learning concepts and Kubernetes architecture. From there, we'll delve into the practical aspects of containerizing machine learning applications, orchestrating complex workflows, deploying models for various use cases, and scaling your applications to meet real-world demands.

This book is not just about theory; it's about empowering you to take action. Throughout each chapter, you'll find hands-on examples, code samples, and real-world use cases that illustrate how Kubernetes can be applied to solve diverse machine learning challenges. We'll also share best practices, tips, and troubleshooting techniques to help you navigate the complexities of this exciting domain.

By the end of this book, you'll be equipped to:

- Set up and configure a Kubernetes environment for machine learning.
- Containerize your machine learning models and dependencies.
- Build and orchestrate complex machine learning workflows.
- Deploy models for various use cases, including real-time prediction and batch processing.
- Scale your machine learning applications to handle increasing demands.
- Manage and monitor your deployments for optimal performance and reliability.
- Secure your Kubernetes cluster and protect sensitive data.
- Explore advanced topics such as serverless machine learning and edge AI.

We believe that Kubernetes has the potential to revolutionize the way machine learning applications are developed and deployed. This book is your guide to unlocking that potential, empowering you to build intelligent applications that are scalable, reliable, and ready to transform the world around us.

We invite you to embark on this journey with us, and we hope that this book will be a valuable resource on your path to mastering machine learning with Kubernetes.

Chapter 1: Introduction

You've picked up this book because you're interested in the exciting intersection of machine learning (ML) and Kubernetes. Maybe you're a seasoned ML practitioner looking for better ways to deploy your models, or perhaps you're a Kubernetes enthusiast eager to explore its potential for AI. Wherever you're coming from, you're in the right place. This chapter sets the stage for our journey, exploring why this combination is so powerful and giving you a roadmap for the adventure ahead.

1.1 Convergence of Machine Learning and Kubernetes

You and I both know that the world of technology is changing rapidly. Two of the biggest forces driving this change are machine learning and Kubernetes. Let's explore how these two powerful technologies are coming together to reshape the way we build and deploy software.

Machine learning, as you probably know, is a type of artificial intelligence that allows computers to learn from data without being explicitly programmed. It's used in a wide range of applications, from self-driving cars to fraud detection.

Kubernetes, on the other hand, is a powerful open-source system for automating the deployment, scaling, and management of containerized applications. It's become the de facto standard for orchestrating applications in the cloud.

Now, you might be wondering, what do these two seemingly disparate technologies have to do with each other? Well, it turns out they complement each other beautifully. Let me explain.

Challenges of Machine Learning in Production

Developing a machine learning model is just the first step. To be truly useful, that model needs to be deployed into a production environment where it can interact with real-world data and generate valuable insights. But deploying and managing ML models in production can be tricky.

Here are some of the challenges:

- Complex Dependencies: ML models often rely on a complex stack of software libraries and frameworks. Managing these dependencies and ensuring they work correctly together can be a headache.
- Resource Intensive: Training and running ML models can require significant computing resources, especially for complex models and large datasets.
- Scalability: The demand for ML models can fluctuate greatly. You need a system that can scale up or down quickly to handle these changes.
- Reproducibility: It's essential to be able to reproduce your ML experiments and deployments to ensure consistency and reliability.

How Kubernetes Addresses These Challenges

This is where Kubernetes shines. It provides a robust and flexible platform for addressing the challenges of deploying and managing machine learning models in production.

Let's look at how Kubernetes tackles each of these challenges:

- Dependency Management: Kubernetes uses containers to package your ML models and their dependencies. This ensures that your models run consistently across different environments.
- Resource Management: Kubernetes allows you to specify the resource requirements for your ML workloads (CPU,

memory, GPU). It then schedules your workloads efficiently across your cluster, ensuring that they have the resources they need to run effectively.
- Scalability: Kubernetes makes it easy to scale your ML applications up or down based on demand. You can configure Kubernetes to automatically adjust the number of replicas of your application based on metrics like CPU usage or request volume.
- Reproducibility: Kubernetes allows you to define your ML deployments declaratively using YAML files. This makes it easy to recreate your deployments and ensures consistency across different environments.

A Practical Example: Deploying a TensorFlow Model with Kubernetes

Let's see a concrete example of how you can use Kubernetes to deploy a TensorFlow model.

First, you'll need to package your TensorFlow model and its dependencies into a Docker image. Here's a simple Dockerfile:

```
Dockerfile

FROM tensorflow/tensorflow:latest

WORKDIR /app

COPY model.py .

COPY requirements.txt .

RUN pip install -r requirements.txt

CMD ["python", "model.py"]
```

This Dockerfile starts with a base image that includes TensorFlow. It then copies your model code (model.py) and dependencies (requirements.txt) into the image. Finally, it runs a command to install the dependencies and starts your model.

Next, you'll need to create a Kubernetes deployment to run your Docker image. Here's a simple YAML definition for a deployment:

YAML

```yaml
apiVersion: apps/v1
kind: Deployment
metadata:
  name: tensorflow-model
spec:
  replicas: 3
  selector:
    matchLabels:
      app: tensorflow-model
  template:
    metadata:
      labels:
        app: tensorflow-model
    spec:
      containers:
      - name: tensorflow-model
```
[1]

```yaml
    image: <your-docker-image>
    ports:
    - containerPort: 8501
```

This deployment will create three replicas of your TensorFlow model, each running in a separate pod. It also exposes your model on port 8501.

Finally, you can create a Kubernetes service to expose your deployment to the outside world. Here's a YAML definition for a service:

YAML

```yaml
apiVersion: v1
kind: Service
metadata:
  name: tensorflow-model-service
spec:
  selector:
    app: tensorflow-model
  ports:
  - protocol: TCP
    port: 80
    targetPort: 8501
  type: LoadBalancer
```

This service will create a load balancer that distributes traffic across the three replicas of your TensorFlow model.

This is just a simple example, of course. Kubernetes offers a wealth of features for managing complex ML deployments, including:

- Autoscaling: Automatically adjust the number of replicas based on demand.
- Health checks: Monitor the health of your pods and restart them if they fail.
- Rolling updates: Deploy new versions of your model without downtime.
- Resource quotas: Limit the resources that your ML workloads can consume.

Real-World Examples

Many companies are already using Kubernetes to power their machine learning initiatives. Here are a few examples:

- Spotify: Uses Kubernetes to train and deploy machine learning models for music recommendation.
- Airbnb: Uses Kubernetes to power its search ranking and fraud detection systems.
- OpenAI: Uses Kubernetes to train and deploy large language models.

The convergence of machine learning and Kubernetes is still in its early stages, but it's clear that these two technologies have the potential to transform the way we build and deploy intelligent applications. As you continue through this book, you'll gain the knowledge and skills you need to harness the power of this exciting combination.

1.2 Why Kubernetes for Machine Learning?

Machine learning workflows often involve a series of complex, interconnected steps. You need to gather and prepare data, train models (often using specialized hardware like GPUs), deploy those models for inference, and continuously monitor their performance. Each of these steps can have unique requirements and challenges.

Kubernetes provides a robust and flexible platform for managing these complexities. It's like having a highly skilled orchestration team that handles the underlying infrastructure and lets you focus on what matters most: building and improving your ML models.

Here's a deeper look at why Kubernetes is a game-changer for machine learning:

1. Tackling the Resource Challenge

Machine learning, particularly deep learning, can be incredibly resource-intensive. Training complex models often requires powerful hardware like GPUs, and even inference (using the model to make predictions) can demand significant computational power.

Kubernetes excels at resource management. Here's how:

- Resource Allocation: You can specify the exact CPU, memory, and GPU resources needed for each stage of your ML workflow. Kubernetes ensures that these resources are allocated efficiently across your cluster.
- Hardware Acceleration: Kubernetes seamlessly integrates with various hardware accelerators like GPUs, TPUs, and FPGAs, allowing you to leverage their power for faster training and inference.
- Resource Optimization: Kubernetes helps you get the most out of your hardware by optimizing resource utilization. It can even automatically scale your applications up or down

based on demand, saving you money on cloud computing costs.

2. Simplifying the Deployment Puzzle

Deploying machine learning models can be a complex process. You need to package your model, its dependencies, and any required runtime environments. Then you need to make it accessible to users or other applications, often through APIs or other interfaces.

Kubernetes simplifies deployment in several ways:

- Containerization: Kubernetes works seamlessly with Docker, the industry-standard containerization technology. You can package your ML model and all its dependencies into a Docker image, ensuring consistency and portability across different environments.
- Service Discovery and Load Balancing: Kubernetes makes it easy to expose your ML models as services with stable network endpoints. It also provides built-in load balancing to distribute traffic across multiple instances of your model, ensuring high availability and fault tolerance.
- Deployment Strategies: Kubernetes supports various deployment strategies, such as rolling updates and canary deployments, allowing you to update your models with minimal disruption to your users.

3. Scaling to Meet Demand

The demand for your ML models can fluctuate significantly. You might experience spikes in traffic during peak hours or when new features are released. Kubernetes provides powerful tools for scaling your applications to meet these demands.

- Horizontal Pod Autoscaler (HPA): The HPA automatically adjusts the number of replicas (copies) of your application based on metrics like CPU usage or request volume. This

ensures that your application can handle varying workloads without manual intervention.
- Vertical Pod Autoscaler (VPA): The VPA automatically adjusts the resource requests and limits for your pods based on their actual usage. This helps to optimize resource allocation and prevent resource contention.

4. Ensuring Reproducibility and Consistency

Reproducibility is crucial in machine learning. You need to be able to recreate your experiments and deployments to ensure consistent results and track changes over time.

Kubernetes helps you achieve reproducibility through:

- Declarative Configuration: You define your desired state in YAML files, which act as blueprints for your deployments. This makes it easy to version your deployments and recreate them in different environments.
- Version Control: You can store your Kubernetes configuration files in a version control system like Git, allowing you to track changes and roll back to previous versions if needed.
- Immutable Infrastructure: Kubernetes encourages the use of immutable infrastructure, where deployments are treated as disposable units. This helps to prevent configuration drift and ensures consistency across your deployments.

5. Accelerating the Development Lifecycle

Kubernetes can significantly speed up your machine learning development lifecycle by providing tools and features that automate many of the tedious tasks associated with building, deploying, and managing ML applications.

- CI/CD Integration: Kubernetes integrates seamlessly with popular CI/CD tools, allowing you to automate your build, test, and deployment pipelines.

- Simplified Rollouts and Rollbacks: Kubernetes makes it easy to deploy new versions of your models and roll back to previous versions if necessary.
- Reduced Operational Overhead: Kubernetes automates many of the operational tasks associated with managing applications, freeing up your team to focus on developing and improving your models.

Real-World Examples

Many leading companies are leveraging Kubernetes to power their machine learning initiatives.

- Airbnb: Uses Kubernetes to manage its machine learning infrastructure, enabling them to scale their models to handle millions of users and listings.
- Spotify: Relies on Kubernetes to deploy and manage its machine learning models for music recommendation and personalization.
- Wayfair: Uses Kubernetes to orchestrate its ML pipelines for tasks like image recognition and product categorization.

These examples demonstrate how Kubernetes can be used to address the unique challenges of deploying and managing machine learning workloads at scale.

Embracing Kubernetes, you can unlock the full potential of your machine learning efforts and build intelligent applications that are robust, scalable, and ready to meet the demands of the modern world.

1.3 Machine Learning Workflow Overview

Before we get our hands dirty with Kubernetes, let's take a step back and look at the bigger picture: the typical machine learning workflow. Understanding this workflow will help you see how Kubernetes fits in and where it can provide the most value.

Think of a machine learning project like baking a cake. You wouldn't just throw all the ingredients in a bowl and hope for the best, right? There's a process, a series of steps you follow to get that delicious outcome. Similarly, a successful machine learning project follows a structured workflow.

1. Data Collection and Preparation

This is where it all starts. You need data to train your machine learning model – the more, the better (usually!). This data can come from various sources: databases, APIs, sensors, files, and more.

But raw data is rarely ready for use. You need to clean it, handle missing values, and format it in a way your model can understand. This might involve:

- Data Cleaning: Removing or correcting errors, inconsistencies, and duplicates.
- Data Transformation: Converting data types, scaling features, and creating new features from existing ones.
- Data Splitting: Dividing the data into training, validation, and test sets.

Example: Let's say you're building a model to predict customer churn. You might collect data from your CRM system, website analytics, and customer support interactions. You'll then need to clean this data by removing duplicate entries, correcting inconsistencies in customer information, and converting categorical variables (like "country") into numerical representations.

2. Feature Engineering

This step is all about selecting, transforming, and creating the features that will be used as input to your model. Think of features as the ingredients that go into your machine learning recipe. The right features can significantly improve your model's accuracy and performance.

Feature engineering might involve:

- Feature Selection: Choosing the most relevant features from your dataset.
- Feature Extraction: Creating new features from existing ones (e.g., combining multiple features or applying mathematical transformations).
- Feature Scaling: Normalizing or standardizing features to a common scale.

Example: In our customer churn example, you might engineer features like "total number of purchases," "average purchase value," "days since last purchase," and "number of support tickets submitted."

3. Model Training

Now it's time to train your machine learning model. This involves feeding your prepared data to a chosen algorithm and letting it learn the patterns and relationships within the data.

You'll typically experiment with different algorithms (linear regression, decision trees, neural networks, etc.) and hyperparameters (settings that control the learning process) to find the best model for your task.

This step often requires significant computing resources, especially for complex models and large datasets. This is where Kubernetes can be particularly helpful, allowing you to distribute training across multiple machines and leverage specialized hardware like GPUs.

Example: You might train a logistic regression model, a support vector machine, and a random forest to predict customer churn.

You'll then evaluate their performance on your validation set to choose the best model.

4. Model Evaluation

Once you have a trained model, you need to evaluate its performance. This involves testing it on a held-out dataset (the test set) that it hasn't seen before.

You'll use various metrics to assess the model's accuracy, precision, recall, and other relevant measures. This evaluation helps you understand how well your model generalizes to new data and identifies areas for improvement.

Example: You might evaluate your churn prediction model using metrics like accuracy, precision, recall, and F1-score. You might also analyze the model's predictions to understand which features are most important for predicting churn.

5. Model Deployment

This is where your model goes live! You need to deploy it in a way that allows users or other applications to access it and make predictions.

There are various deployment patterns for machine learning models:

- Online Inference: The model is deployed as a web service that provides real-time predictions via an API.
- Batch Inference: The model is used to generate predictions on a batch of data, often on a scheduled basis.
- Embedded Inference: The model is embedded within another application or device.

Kubernetes can help you deploy your models in a reliable, scalable, and secure manner.

Example: You might deploy your churn prediction model as a web service that allows your CRM system to access it and get real-time churn predictions for each customer.

6. Monitoring and Maintenance

Deploying your model isn't the end of the story. You need to continuously monitor its performance and make adjustments as needed.

This might involve:

- Performance Monitoring: Tracking metrics like accuracy, latency, and throughput.
- Model Retraining: Retraining your model on new data to maintain its accuracy and adapt to changing patterns.
- Troubleshooting: Identifying and resolving issues that may arise with your deployed model.

Kubernetes provides tools and features that can help you monitor and maintain your ML deployments, ensuring they continue to perform optimally over time.

Example: You might monitor your churn prediction model's accuracy over time and retrain it periodically with new data to ensure it remains effective.

As you can see, Kubernetes can play a crucial role in every stage of the machine learning workflow. It provides a powerful platform for managing the complexities of data preparation, model training, deployment, and monitoring.

By leveraging Kubernetes, you can streamline your ML workflows, accelerate your development lifecycle, and build intelligent applications that are robust, scalable, and ready to meet the demands of the real world.

1.4 Kubernetes Fundamentals

Now that you have a good grasp of the machine learning workflow, let's shift our focus to Kubernetes itself. Think of Kubernetes as the conductor of your machine learning orchestra, coordinating all the different instruments (your applications and services) to create a harmonious symphony.

But before you can conduct, you need to understand the instruments and how they work together. So, let's explore the fundamental concepts and components that make up a Kubernetes system.

1. The Kubernetes Cluster

At the heart of Kubernetes lies the **cluster**. A cluster is a collection of machines, called **nodes**, that work together to run your applications. These nodes can be physical servers, virtual machines in the cloud, or even devices at the edge.

Think of a cluster like a team of workers. Each worker (node) has its own set of skills and resources, and they collaborate to accomplish a shared goal (running your applications).

2. Nodes

Each node in a Kubernetes cluster is a machine that runs your containerized applications. It's responsible for:

- Running containers: Nodes host and execute the containers that make up your applications.
- Managing resources: Nodes track and manage the resources (CPU, memory, storage) available to containers.
- Communicating with the control plane: Nodes communicate with the control plane (which we'll discuss next) to receive instructions and report their status.

3. The Control Plane

The control plane is the brain of the Kubernetes cluster. It's responsible for:

- Managing the cluster state: The control plane maintains a desired state for the cluster, ensuring that the actual state matches the desired state.
- Scheduling workloads: The control plane decides which node to run each application on, based on factors like resource availability and node health.
- Scaling applications: The control plane can automatically scale applications up or down based on demand.
- Monitoring and managing cluster health: The control plane monitors the health of the cluster and its components, taking corrective action if necessary.

The control plane consists of several key components:

- API server: The front door to the Kubernetes cluster. It receives requests from users and other components and interacts with the etcd database to store and retrieve cluster state.
- Scheduler: Assigns pods to nodes based on resource requirements and other constraints.
- Controller manager: Ensures that the actual state of the cluster matches the desired state.
- etcd: A distributed key-value store that stores the cluster state and configuration.

4. Pods: The Building Blocks

In Kubernetes, the smallest deployable unit is a **pod**. A pod is a group of one or more containers that share the same network namespace and storage volumes.

Think of a pod like a container ship. It carries your containers (your application components) and provides them with the necessary resources (network, storage) to function.

5. Deployments

A deployment is a Kubernetes object that manages the rollout and updates of your application. It ensures that the desired number of replicas of your application are running at all times.

Think of a deployment like an automated deployment manager. It takes care of creating, updating, and scaling your application, so you don't have to do it manually.

6. Services

A service is a Kubernetes object that provides a stable network endpoint for accessing your application. It acts as an abstraction layer, decoupling your application from its underlying pods.

Think of a service like a receptionist. It directs incoming requests to the appropriate pods, even if those pods are moved or replaced.

7. Namespaces

A namespace is a way to divide your Kubernetes cluster into logical partitions. You can use namespaces to isolate different teams, projects, or environments.

Think of namespaces like separate departments within a company. Each department has its own resources and can operate independently without interfering with other departments.

Working with Kubernetes: YAML and kubectl

You interact with Kubernetes using YAML files and the kubectl command-line tool.

YAML: You use YAML files to define your Kubernetes objects, such as pods, deployments, and services. Here's an example of a simple YAML file for a deployment:

YAML

```yaml
apiVersion: apps/v1
kind: Deployment
metadata:
  name: my-app
spec:
  replicas: 3
  selector:
    matchLabels:
      app: my-app
  template:
    metadata:
      labels:
        app: my-app
    spec:
      containers:
      - name: my-app
        image:[1] nginx:latest
        ports:
        - containerPort:[2] 80
```

This YAML file defines a deployment named my-app that creates three replicas of a pod running the nginx:latest image.

kubectl: kubectl is a command-line tool that allows you to interact with your Kubernetes cluster. You can use kubectl to create, update, delete, and inspect Kubernetes objects.

For example, to create the deployment defined in the YAML file above, you would use the following command:

Bash

```
kubectl apply -f deployment.yaml
```

Real-World Examples

Kubernetes is used by many organizations to manage their applications, including:

- Pokémon Go: Niantic uses Kubernetes to manage the massive scale of Pokémon Go, handling millions of users worldwide.
- New York Times: The New York Times uses Kubernetes to run its website and other digital properties.
- Spotify: Spotify uses Kubernetes to manage its music streaming service, ensuring high availability and scalability.

Understanding these Kubernetes fundamentals, you'll be well-equipped to start using it for your machine learning projects. In the next chapter, we'll get hands-on and start setting up your Kubernetes environment.

1.5 Book Structure and Conventions

This book is structured to provide a progressive learning experience, starting with the essentials and gradually building up to more advanced topics. We'll use a hands-on approach, with plenty of practical examples and code samples to help you solidify your understanding.

Part I: Foundations

This part lays the groundwork for your journey with Kubernetes and machine learning. We'll cover:

- Setting up your Kubernetes environment: We'll guide you through the process of setting up a Kubernetes cluster, whether you prefer a local environment like Minikube or a cloud-based solution like Google Kubernetes Engine (GKE), Amazon Elastic Kubernetes Service (EKS), or Azure Kubernetes Service (AKS). You'll learn how to interact with your cluster using the kubectl command-line tool.
- Containerizing machine learning applications: We'll introduce you to Docker, the popular containerization technology, and show you how to package your machine learning models and their dependencies into Docker images. This ensures portability and consistency across different environments.
- Kubernetes core concepts: We'll explore the essential building blocks of Kubernetes, including pods, deployments, services, and namespaces. You'll learn how these components work together to orchestrate your applications.

Part II: Building and Deploying

In this part, we'll roll up our sleeves and start building and deploying machine learning workflows on Kubernetes. We'll cover:

- Building machine learning workflows: You'll learn how to orchestrate complex machine learning pipelines on Kubernetes, including data preprocessing, model training, and evaluation. We'll explore tools like Argo and Kubeflow that can help you manage these workflows effectively.

- Deploying machine learning models: We'll examine different deployment patterns for machine learning models, including online inference (real-time predictions via APIs), batch inference (processing large datasets), and embedded inference (integrating models into other applications). You'll learn how to expose your models using Kubernetes services and ingress.
- Scaling and resource management: We'll discuss how to scale your machine learning applications to handle varying workloads and optimize resource utilization. You'll learn about techniques like horizontal pod autoscaling (HPA) and vertical pod autoscaling (VPA).

Part III: Managing and Advanced Topics

This part explores more advanced topics and best practices for managing and securing your machine learning deployments on Kubernetes. We'll cover:

- Managing machine learning pipelines: You'll learn how to manage the entire lifecycle of your machine learning pipelines, including version control, experiment tracking, and model promotion. We'll explore tools and techniques for continuous integration and continuous delivery (CI/CD) for machine learning.
- Security and access control: We'll discuss how to secure your Kubernetes cluster and your machine learning applications. You'll learn about authentication, authorization, and best practices for protecting sensitive data.
- Advanced topics and future trends: We'll touch on advanced topics like serverless machine learning with Knative, using GPUs and other hardware accelerators, and exploring emerging trends like federated learning and edge AI.

Conventions Used in This Book

To ensure clarity and consistency, we'll use the following conventions throughout this book:

- Code examples: Code examples will be presented in a monospace font. We'll use syntax highlighting to improve readability.
- Command-line instructions: Commands that you should execute in your terminal will be prefixed with a dollar sign ($). For example:

Bash

```
$ kubectl get pods
```

- File names and paths: File names and paths will be presented in italics. For example: *deployment.yaml*.
- Important terms: Key terms will be highlighted in bold when they are first introduced.
- Tips and best practices: We'll provide helpful tips and best practices throughout the book to help you avoid common pitfalls and get the most out of Kubernetes.

Exercises

At the end of some chapters, you'll find exercises to help you reinforce your learning and apply the concepts you've learned. These exercises are designed to be practical and challenging, encouraging you to experiment and explore.

Real-World Examples

We'll use real-world examples throughout the book to illustrate how Kubernetes is being used by companies and organizations to solve real-world machine learning challenges. These examples will provide you with valuable insights and inspiration.

A Note on Prerequisites

While this book is designed to be accessible to a wide audience, some basic familiarity with Linux, command-line interfaces, and programming concepts will be helpful. Don't worry if you're not an expert in these areas – we'll provide clear explanations and guidance along the way.

Let's Get Started!

We're excited to embark on this journey with you! In the next chapter, we'll start by setting up your Kubernetes environment and getting your hands dirty with the `kubectl` command-line tool.

Chapter 2: Setting Up Your Kubernetes Environment

In this chapter, we'll walk through the process of setting up your very own Kubernetes environment. Think of this as building your machine learning laboratory – a dedicated space where you can experiment, build, and deploy your amazing AI creations.

2.1 Choosing a Kubernetes Distribution

The first step in our Kubernetes journey is choosing the right distribution. Think of it like selecting the perfect car for your needs. Do you need a compact car for zipping around the city, a powerful truck for hauling heavy loads, or a luxurious sedan for cruising in comfort?

Similarly, different Kubernetes distributions cater to different needs and use cases. Let's explore some of the most popular options and help you find the perfect fit for your machine learning adventures.

1. Minikube

Minikube is like that trusty bicycle you had as a kid. It's simple, reliable, and perfect for exploring your neighborhood (in this case, the world of Kubernetes). It sets up a single-node Kubernetes cluster right on your laptop or desktop, making it ideal for:

- Learning Kubernetes: Minikube provides a hassle-free way to experiment with Kubernetes concepts, try out different configurations, and get comfortable with the command-line interface (kubectl).
- Developing locally: You can use Minikube to develop and test your machine learning applications locally before

deploying them to a production environment. This allows you to iterate quickly and catch errors early on.
- Resource-constrained environments: If you're working on a machine with limited resources, Minikube's lightweight footprint makes it a great choice.

How Minikube Works

Minikube leverages virtualization technology (like VirtualBox or Hyper-V) to create a virtual machine on your local machine. This virtual machine hosts all the Kubernetes components, including the control plane and the worker node.

Getting Started with Minikube

Installing Minikube is a breeze. You can download the binary for your operating system from the official Minikube website and follow the simple installation instructions.

Once installed, you can start a Minikube cluster with a single command:

```
Bash
```

```
$ minikube start
```

This command will download a pre-built virtual machine image, start the virtual machine, and configure kubectl to connect to the cluster.

2. Kind: Kubernetes in Docker

Kind (Kubernetes in Docker) takes a slightly different approach. It runs a Kubernetes cluster inside a Docker container. This offers some unique advantages:

- Portability: Since Kind runs within Docker, you can easily move your cluster between different environments. This is

especially useful if you're working with different operating systems or cloud providers.
- Efficiency: Kind is very resource-efficient, as it leverages Docker's existing infrastructure.
- Reproducibility: Kind makes it easy to create reproducible Kubernetes environments, which is crucial for testing and development.

How Kind Works

Kind uses Docker to create a container that acts as a node in your Kubernetes cluster. Multiple containers can be networked together to form a multi-node cluster.

Getting Started with Kind

To use Kind, you'll need to have Docker installed on your machine. You can then download the Kind binary and create a cluster with a single command:

```bash
$ kind create cluster
```

This command will create a local Kubernetes cluster running inside a Docker container.

3. Managed Kubernetes in the Cloud

If you're serious about machine learning and need a robust, scalable, and production-ready environment, you should consider a managed Kubernetes service from a cloud provider. These services offer several benefits:

- Scalability and Reliability: Cloud providers have massive infrastructure and expertise to ensure your Kubernetes cluster can handle demanding workloads and remain highly available.

- Simplified Management: Managed services take care of the underlying infrastructure, including node management, upgrades, and security patching. This frees you up to focus on your applications.
- Integration with Cloud Services: Managed Kubernetes services seamlessly integrate with other cloud services, such as storage, databases, and monitoring tools.

Let's look at the leading managed Kubernetes offerings:

- Google Kubernetes Engine (GKE): GKE is a fully managed Kubernetes service from Google Cloud Platform. It's known for its strong integration with other Google Cloud services, its advanced features like auto-scaling and auto-repair, and its focus on developer experience.
- Amazon Elastic Kubernetes Service (EKS): EKS is Amazon Web Services' managed Kubernetes offering. It's a solid choice if you're already using AWS and want a seamless integration with their ecosystem. EKS is also known for its security features and compliance certifications.
- Azure Kubernetes Service (AKS): AKS is Microsoft Azure's managed Kubernetes service. It offers a good balance of features, performance, and cost-effectiveness. AKS is also well-integrated with other Azure services and offers strong support for Windows workloads.

Getting Started with Managed Kubernetes

Each cloud provider has its own process for creating and managing Kubernetes clusters. You'll typically use their web console or command-line interface to create a cluster, configure its settings, and deploy your applications.

Which One Should You Choose?

The best choice for you will depend on your specific needs and preferences. Here's a quick guide:

- **For learning and local development:** Minikube or Kind are excellent choices.
- **For production deployments or when you need more resources:** A managed Kubernetes service like GKE, EKS, or AKS is recommended.
- **Consider your existing cloud provider:** If you're already using a particular cloud provider, it often makes sense to choose their managed Kubernetes service for seamless integration.

In this book, we'll primarily use Minikube for its simplicity and ease of use. However, the concepts and techniques you learn will be applicable to any Kubernetes distribution.

Choosing the right Kubernetes distribution is an important first step in your journey. Take some time to consider your needs, explore the different options, and choose the one that best fits your machine learning goals. In the next section, we'll install kubectl, the command-line tool you'll use to interact with your cluster.

2.2 Installing and Configuring kubectl

Now that you've chosen your Kubernetes distribution, it's time to install and configure kubectl, your command-line interface to the Kubernetes cluster. Think of kubectl as your trusty Swiss Army knife for managing and interacting with your Kubernetes environment.

With kubectl, you can:

- Create, update, and delete Kubernetes resources: This includes everything from deploying applications and services to managing network configurations and storage volumes.
- Inspect the state of your cluster: You can get detailed information about the nodes, pods, and other resources running in your cluster.

- Troubleshoot issues: kubectl provides powerful tools for diagnosing and resolving problems in your Kubernetes environment.
- Execute commands in your containers: You can use kubectl to access the command line of your running containers, which is useful for debugging and troubleshooting.

In short, kubectl is an essential tool for anyone working with Kubernetes. Let's get it installed and configured on your system.

Installing kubectl

The installation process for kubectl is generally straightforward, but it can vary slightly depending on your operating system. Here's a general overview of the steps involved:

1. **Download the kubectl binary:** You can download the latest release of kubectl from the official Kubernetes website. Make sure to choose the binary that matches your operating system and architecture.
2. **Make the binary executable:** Once you've downloaded the binary, you'll need to make it executable. You can do this using the chmod command in your terminal:

Bash

```
$ chmod +x kubectl
```

3. **Move the binary to your PATH:** To be able to run kubectl from any directory in your terminal, you need to move it to a directory that's included in your system's PATH environment variable. A common location is /usr/local/bin:

Bash

```
$ sudo mv kubectl /usr/local/bin
```

4. **Verify the installation:** You can verify that kubectl is installed correctly by running the following command:

```Bash

$ kubectl version
```

This should display the client and server versions of kubectl.

Configuring kubectl

Once kubectl is installed, you need to configure it to connect to your Kubernetes cluster. This involves setting up a kubeconfig file, which contains the necessary credentials and configuration information.

The process for obtaining and configuring your kubeconfig file depends on your chosen Kubernetes distribution:

Minikube:

- When you start a Minikube cluster using the minikube start command, it automatically configures kubectl to connect to it. You don't need to do anything else.

Kind:

- Similarly, Kind automatically configures kubectl when you create a cluster using the kind create cluster command.

Managed Kubernetes services (GKE, EKS, AKS):

- Each cloud provider has its own process for generating and downloading kubeconfig files. You'll typically find this option in your cloud console or through their command-line interface.

- Once you have the kubeconfig file, you can configure kubectl to use it by setting the KUBECONFIG environment variable:

Bash

```
$ export KUBECONFIG=/path/to/your/kubeconfig
```

Alternatively, you can use the kubectl config use-context command to switch between different kubeconfig files.

Verifying the Configuration

To verify that kubectl is correctly configured to connect to your cluster, you can run the following command:

Bash

```
$ kubectl cluster-info
```

This should display information about your cluster, including its name, server address, and version. If you see an error message, double-check your kubeconfig file and ensure your cluster is running.

kubectl Context and Configuration

It's worth noting that kubectl can manage connections to multiple clusters. Each cluster connection is represented by a "context" in your kubeconfig file. You can switch between different contexts using the kubectl config use-context command. This is useful if you're working with multiple clusters, such as a local development cluster and a production cluster in the cloud.

Troubleshooting kubectl Configuration

If you encounter issues with your kubectl configuration, here are a few things to check:

- File permissions: Ensure that your kubeconfig file has the correct permissions. You might need to use the chmod command to adjust the permissions.
- File format: Make sure your kubeconfig file is in the correct format. It should be a valid YAML file.
- Cluster connectivity: Ensure that your machine can reach the Kubernetes API server. This might involve configuring network firewalls or proxy settings.
- Authentication credentials: Verify that the authentication credentials in your kubeconfig file are valid.

With kubectl installed and configured, you now have the power to control and manage your Kubernetes cluster. In the next section, we'll explore some fundamental Kubernetes concepts that will be essential for deploying your machine learning applications.

2.3 Understanding Kubernetes Concepts

These concepts are fundamental to understanding how Kubernetes orchestrates and manages your applications, including your future machine learning deployments. Think of these concepts as the essential vocabulary of Kubernetes. Once you grasp them, you'll be able to speak the language fluently and build sophisticated applications with confidence.

Pods

In Kubernetes, the most basic unit of deployment is the **Pod**. It's the smallest and simplest object you can create and manage.

Think of a pod as a container ship carrying your application. It provides the environment and resources for your containers to run. A pod can hold one or more containers that are tightly coupled and share resources like storage and network.

Why use Pods?

- Co-location: Pods allow you to group containers that need to work closely together. For example, your main application container might be paired with a "sidecar" container that handles logging or configuration updates.
- Resource sharing: Containers within a pod share the same network namespace, allowing them to communicate easily with each other. They can also share storage volumes.
- Simplified management: Kubernetes manages pods as a single unit, making it easier to deploy, scale, and monitor your applications.

Pod Lifecycle

Pods have a life cycle that includes several states:

- Pending: The pod has been created but not yet scheduled to a node.
- Running: The pod has been scheduled to a node and all its containers are running.
- Succeeded: All containers in the pod have terminated successfully.
- Failed: One or more containers in the pod have terminated with a failure.
- Unknown: The state of the pod cannot be determined.

Kubernetes constantly monitors the state of your pods and takes action to maintain the desired state. For example, if a pod fails, Kubernetes will automatically try to restart it.

Deployments

While you can create individual pods directly, you'll typically use Deployments to manage them. A Deployment is a higher-level object that provides declarative updates for Pods and ReplicaSets.

Think of a Deployment as a supervisor for your pods. It ensures that the desired number of replicas of your application are running at all times, even if pods fail or nodes become unavailable.

Key features of Deployments:

- Rolling updates: Deployments can perform rolling updates, gradually replacing old pods with new ones without any downtime.
- Rollbacks: If a deployment fails, you can easily roll it back to a previous version.
- Scaling: You can easily scale your application up or down by changing the number of replicas in the Deployment.
- Self-healing: Deployments automatically restart failed pods and ensure that the desired state is maintained.

Services

A Service in Kubernetes provides a stable network endpoint for accessing your application. It acts as an abstraction layer, decoupling your application from its underlying pods. This means that even if pods are moved or replaced, the service remains accessible at the same IP address and port.

Why use Services?

- Stable endpoint: Services provide a consistent way to access your application, regardless of how many pods are running or where they are located.
- Load balancing: Services can distribute traffic across multiple pods, ensuring high availability and fault tolerance.
- Service discovery: Services make it easy for applications within the cluster to find and communicate with each other.

Types of Services

Kubernetes offers different types of services, each with its own characteristics:

- ClusterIP: Exposes the service on a cluster-internal IP. This is the default type.
- NodePort: Exposes the service on each node's IP at a static port.
- LoadBalancer: Exposes the service externally using a cloud provider's load balancer.
- ExternalName: Maps the service to1 an external DNS name.

Namespaces

As your Kubernetes cluster grows, you might want to divide it into logical partitions to organize your resources and control access. This is where Namespaces come in.

Think of namespaces as separate compartments within your cluster. Each namespace provides a scope for names. This means you can have resources with the same name in different namespaces without any conflicts.

Why use Namespaces?

- Resource isolation: Namespaces allow you to isolate resources for different teams, projects, or environments.
- Access control: You can use namespaces to control access to resources, ensuring that only authorized users can access them.
- Resource quotas: You can set resource quotas for each namespace, limiting the amount of resources that can be consumed.

Working with these Concepts

Throughout this book, you'll see these concepts in action as we build and deploy machine learning applications. You'll learn how to define pods, deployments, and services using YAML files and manage them using *kubectl*.

Real-World Examples

These Kubernetes concepts are used extensively in real-world applications:

- E-commerce platforms: Companies like Amazon and eBay use Kubernetes to manage their massive e-commerce platforms, ensuring high availability and scalability.
- Financial institutions: Banks and other financial institutions use Kubernetes to run their critical applications, ensuring security and compliance.
- Gaming companies: Gaming companies like Blizzard use Kubernetes to manage their online games, handling millions of concurrent players.

Understanding these core concepts, you'll be well-equipped to navigate the world of Kubernetes and build robust and scalable machine learning applications. In the next section, we'll take a closer look at how to work with Kubernetes resources using YAML and kubectl.

2.4 Working with Kubernetes Resources

Kubernetes is like a sophisticated machine with many levers and buttons. To operate this machine effectively, you need to understand its control panel. In the Kubernetes world, that control panel is a combination of YAML files and the kubectl command-line tool.

YAML

YAML (YAML Ain't Markup Language) is a human-readable data serialization language. It's often used for configuration files and in applications where data is being stored or transmitted.[1] In Kubernetes, you use YAML files to define your desired state. This means you describe what you want your application to look like—how many pods it should have, what container image to use, what ports to expose, and so on.

Here's a simple example of a YAML file that defines a Deployment:

YAML

```yaml
apiVersion: apps/v1
kind: Deployment
metadata:
  name: my-app
spec:
  replicas: 3
  selector:
    matchLabels:
      app: my-app
  template:
    metadata:
      labels:
        app: my-app
    spec:
      containers:
      - name: my-app
        image:[2] nginx:latest
        ports:
```

```
    - containerPort:³ 80
```

Let's break down this YAML file:

- apiVersion: This specifies the Kubernetes API version used to create this object.
- kind: This indicates the type of Kubernetes resource you're defining (in this case, a Deployment).
- metadata: This section contains metadata about the object, such as its name and labels.
- spec: This section defines the desired state of the object. In this case, we're specifying that we want three replicas of our application, each running the nginx:latest container image.

kubectl: Command-Line Control Center

kubectl is your command-line tool for interacting with the Kubernetes API. It allows you to create, update, delete, and inspect Kubernetes resources.

Here are some essential kubectl commands you'll frequently use:

- kubectl apply -f <filename>: Creates or updates resources defined in a YAML file.
- kubectl get <resource-type>: Lists all resources of a specific type (e.g., kubectl get pods).
- kubectl describe <resource-type> <resource-name>: Provides detailed information about a specific resource.
- kubectl delete <resource-type> <resource-name>: Deletes a resource.
- kubectl logs <pod-name>: Displays the logs of a pod.
- kubectl exec -it <pod-name> -- <command>: Executes a command inside a pod.

A Practical Example

Let's say you want to deploy a simple web application to your Kubernetes cluster. You have a Docker image named my-web-app that contains your application code.

1. **Create a YAML file:** Create a file named deployment.yaml with the following content:

YAML

```yaml
apiVersion: apps/v1
kind: Deployment
metadata:
  name: my-web-app
spec:
  replicas: 2
  selector:
    matchLabels:
      app: my-web-app
  template:
    metadata:
      labels:
        app: my-web-app
    spec:
      containers:
```

```
    - name: my-web-app

      image: my-web-app:latest⁴

      ports:

      - containerPort:⁵ 8080
```

2. **Apply the YAML file:** Use kubectl to create the Deployment:

Bash

```
$ kubectl apply -f deployment.yaml
```

3. **Verify the deployment:** Check that your pods are running:

Bash

```
$ kubectl get pods
```

4. **Expose the application:** Create a Service to expose your application:

YAML

```
apiVersion: v1

kind: Service

metadata:

  name: my-web-app-service

spec:
```

```
selector:
  app: my-web-app
ports:
- protocol: TCP
  port: 80
  targetPort: 8080
type: LoadBalancer
```
[6]

5. Apply the service:

Bash

```
$ kubectl apply -f service.yaml
```

6. **Access your application:** If you're using a managed Kubernetes service, you can get the external IP address of your service using kubectl get service my-web-app-service. You can then access your application in your web browser using this IP address.

This is just a glimpse of what you can do with YAML and kubectl. As you become more familiar with Kubernetes, you'll discover a wealth of commands and options for managing your applications and cluster.

Real-World Examples

YAML and kubectl are used extensively by developers and operations teams to manage Kubernetes deployments in real-world scenarios. Here are a few examples:

- Continuous integration and continuous delivery (CI/CD): YAML files can be used to define entire deployment pipelines, allowing for automated testing and deployment of applications.
- Infrastructure as code: Kubernetes configurations can be managed as code, allowing for version control, collaboration, and reproducibility.
- Automated deployments: kubectl can be used to automate deployments, scaling, and other management tasks, reducing manual effort and improving efficiency.

Mastering YAML and kubectl, you'll be well-equipped to manage your machine learning deployments on Kubernetes effectively and efficiently. In the next section, we'll discuss some common troubleshooting techniques for your Kubernetes setup.

2.5 Troubleshooting and Debugging

Even the most carefully planned Kubernetes setups can sometimes hit a snag. It's like embarking on a road trip – even with the best map and a well-maintained car, you might encounter a flat tire or a detour.

But don't worry! Just like a seasoned traveler, you can learn to diagnose and fix common Kubernetes issues. This section equips you with the troubleshooting skills to get your Kubernetes environment back on track smoothly.

Common Issues and Solutions

Let's explore some of the most frequent problems you might encounter and how to tackle them:

1. kubectl **Not Found**

This error usually means that kubectl isn't installed correctly or isn't in your system's PATH.

Solution:

- Double-check that you've followed the installation instructions for your operating system.
- Verify that the kubectl binary is in a directory listed in your PATH environment variable. You can check your PATH by running echo $PATH in your terminal.
- If you're still having trouble, try reinstalling kubectl.

2. Cannot Connect to the Cluster

This error indicates that kubectl can't communicate with your Kubernetes API server.

Solution:

- Verify cluster status: Make sure your cluster is actually running. If you're using Minikube, run minikube status to check. For cloud-managed clusters, check your cloud provider's console.
- Check kubeconfig: Ensure your kubeconfig file is correctly configured and points to the right cluster. You might need to regenerate the file or update its contents.
- Network connectivity: Make sure your machine can reach the Kubernetes API server. This might involve checking your network firewall, proxy settings, or VPN connection.

3. Pods Are Not Starting

If your pods are stuck in a "Pending" state or are failing to start, there might be several reasons:

- Insufficient resources: Your cluster might not have enough resources (CPU, memory) to schedule the pod. Try increasing the resources requested in your pod's YAML definition.
- Image pull errors: Kubernetes might be unable to pull the container image from the registry. Check the image name

and tag in your YAML file and ensure you have network connectivity to the registry.
- Application errors: There might be errors in your application code that are preventing the container from starting. Check the pod's logs using kubectl logs <pod-name> to identify any error messages.

4. Services Are Not Accessible

If you're unable to access your application through its service, there could be a few culprits:

- Service definition: Double-check that your service is correctly defined in your YAML file. Ensure the selector matches the labels of your pods and that the port and targetPort are correctly specified.
- Network configuration: Verify that your network configuration allows traffic to reach your service. This might involve checking your firewall rules, load balancer settings, or ingress configuration.
- Application issues: There might be issues within your application itself that are preventing it from responding to requests. Check your application logs for any errors.

5. Persistent Volume Claims Not Binding

If you're using Persistent Volumes to store data, you might encounter issues with Persistent Volume Claims (PVCs) not binding to available volumes.

Solution

- Storage class: Ensure that you have a Storage Class defined that matches the requirements of your PVC.
- Available capacity: Check that you have enough storage capacity available in your cluster to provision the volume.

- Access modes: Verify that the access modes requested in your PVC are supported by the available Persistent Volumes.

Debugging Techniques

Here are some essential debugging techniques that can help you pinpoint the cause of problems in your Kubernetes setup:

- kubectl describe: Use the kubectl describe command to get detailed information about a resource, including its events, status, and configuration. This can often reveal the cause of an issue.
- kubectl logs: Examine the logs of your pods using kubectl logs <pod-name>. This can help you identify errors in your application code or configuration.
- kubectl exec: Use kubectl exec -it <pod-name> -- <command> to execute commands inside a pod. This can be useful for debugging your application or inspecting its environment.
- Events: Kubernetes generates events that provide insights into the activities happening in your cluster. You can view events using kubectl get events.
- Monitoring tools: Consider using monitoring tools like Prometheus and Grafana to collect and visualize metrics about your cluster and applications. This can help you identify performance bottlenecks and other issues.

Real-World Examples

Troubleshooting Kubernetes issues is a common task for developers and operations teams. Here are a few real-world scenarios:

- A pod fails to start due to a missing dependency: A developer deploys an application to Kubernetes, but the pod fails to start because a required library is missing from the

container image. By examining the pod's logs, the developer identifies the missing dependency and rebuilds the image to include it.
- A service is inaccessible due to a firewall rule: An operations team deploys a new service to Kubernetes, but it's inaccessible from outside the cluster. They discover that a firewall rule is blocking traffic to the service's port and update the rule to allow access.
- A cluster experiences resource contention: A machine learning engineer trains a large model on Kubernetes, but other applications on the cluster start experiencing performance issues. By monitoring resource usage, the engineer identifies that the model training is consuming excessive resources and adjusts the resource requests and limits to prevent contention.

Troubleshooting Kubernetes can be challenging at times, but it's an essential skill for anyone working with this powerful platform. By understanding common issues and mastering debugging techniques, you can confidently manage your Kubernetes environment and ensure your machine learning applications run smoothly.

Chapter 3: Containerizing Machine Learning Applications

In this chapter, we'll explore the magic of containerization and how it can revolutionize your machine learning workflows. Think of containers as lightweight, portable capsules that encapsulate your entire application, including your code, libraries, and dependencies. It's like having a self-contained mini-environment where your application can run consistently, no matter where it's deployed.

3.1 Introduction to Docker and Containerization

Let's talk about containers! They're a game-changer in the world of software development, and they're especially powerful when it comes to machine learning. Think of containers as lightweight, self-contained packages that hold everything your application needs to run: your code, libraries, dependencies, and even the operating system.

It's like having a complete, miniature computer within your computer, dedicated solely to running your application. This "mini-computer" is isolated from the rest of your system, ensuring consistency and preventing conflicts.

Well, machine learning projects often involve a complex web of dependencies. You might have specific versions of Python libraries, machine learning frameworks like TensorFlow or PyTorch, and even specialized hardware requirements like GPUs. Trying to recreate this exact environment on different machines (your laptop, a testing server, a cloud provider) can be a real nightmare.

This is where containerization comes to the rescue. By packaging your entire application and its dependencies into a container, you ensure that it runs the same way, regardless of the underlying infrastructure. It's like having a magic box that guarantees your application will behave consistently wherever you take it.

Docker

Docker is the most popular containerization platform. It provides tools for building, sharing, and running containers. Think of Docker as the shipping company that handles your containerized applications. It provides the infrastructure and tools to build your containers (like a shipyard), transport them (like cargo ships), and run them wherever you need them (like ports).

Key Benefits of Containerization with Docker for Machine Learning

Let's break down the specific advantages Docker brings to your machine learning projects:

- Portability: This is a huge one! You can build your machine learning application on your laptop, package it into a Docker container, and then deploy it to a cloud cluster without any changes. This eliminates the "it works on my machine" problem and ensures consistency across different environments.
- Reproducibility: With Docker, you can capture the exact state of your application environment, including all dependencies and configurations. This ensures that your experiments and deployments are reproducible, giving you confidence in your results.
- Efficiency: Docker containers are lightweight because they share the host operating system's kernel. This means they consume fewer resources compared to traditional virtual machines, making them more efficient and cost-effective.

- Isolation: Docker containers provide isolation between applications, preventing conflicts and dependency issues. This is crucial in machine learning, where different projects might require different versions of the same libraries.
- Scalability: Docker containers are easy to scale up or down. This is essential for machine learning applications, which often need to handle varying workloads and traffic demands.
- Simplified Collaboration: Docker images can be easily shared through container registries like Docker Hub. This makes it easy to collaborate on machine learning projects and share pre-built environments.

How Docker Works

Docker uses the host operating system's kernel but provides isolated user spaces called containers. Each container has its own file system, network, and processes, making it appear like a separate, self-contained system.

Key Docker Components

- Docker Engine: The core of Docker, responsible for building, running, and managing containers.
- Docker Image: A read-only template that contains everything needed to create a container.
- Docker Container: A running instance of a Docker image.
- Docker Hub: A public registry for storing and sharing Docker images.

Real-World Examples

Many companies leverage Docker to power their machine learning initiatives:

- Spotify: Uses Docker to package and deploy its machine learning models for music recommendation and personalization.

- Airbnb: Uses Docker to containerize its fraud detection and search ranking algorithms, ensuring consistency and scalability.
- Pinterest: Uses Docker to deploy its machine learning models for image recognition and content recommendation.

Embracing Docker and containerization, you're setting the stage for efficient, portable, and reproducible machine learning workflows. In the next section, we'll learn how to build Docker images specifically for your machine learning applications.

3.2 Building Docker Images for Machine Learning

Think of a Docker image as a blueprint for your application's environment. It contains everything needed to run your application: the code, libraries, dependencies, and even the operating system.

To create a Docker image, you use a special file called a Dockerfile. This file contains a set of instructions that tell Docker how to build the image. It's like a recipe that Docker follows step-by-step to create your containerized application.

Anatomy of a Dockerfile

Let's break down the typical structure of a Dockerfile for a machine learning application:

1. FROM: This instruction specifies the base image for your container. You'll often start with an official image that contains the necessary operating system and language runtime (e.g., python:3.9 for a Python 3.9 environment).
2. WORKDIR: This sets the working directory inside the container. It's where your application code and files will reside.

3. **COPY**: This instruction copies files and directories from your local machine into the container image. You'll use this to copy your application code, model files, and other necessary assets.
4. **RUN**: This instruction executes commands inside the container during the build process. You'll use this to install dependencies, set environment variables, and perform other setup tasks.
5. **CMD**: This instruction specifies the command to run when the container starts. This is typically the command to launch your application.

Example: Building a Docker Image for a Scikit-learn Model

Let's say you have a machine learning model built with Scikit-learn that you want to deploy. Here's an example of a Dockerfile you could use:

`Dockerfile`

```
FROM python:3.9-slim

WORKDIR /app

COPY requirements.txt .

RUN pip install -r requirements.txt

COPY model.pkl .

COPY app.py .

CMD ["python", "app.py"]
```

In this Dockerfile:

- We start with a slim Python 3.9 base image (python:3.9-slim) to minimize image size.
- We set the working directory to /app.
- We copy the requirements.txt file, which lists our Python dependencies, and install them using pip.
- We copy the trained model file (model.pkl) and the application code (app.py) into the container.
- We set the command to run when the container starts to python app.py, which will launch our application.

Building the Image

To build this Docker image, you would use the following command in your terminal:

Bash

```
$ docker build -t my-sklearn-app .
```

This command tells Docker to build an image named my-sklearn-app using the Dockerfile in the current directory (.).

Running the Container

Once the image is built, you can run it as a container using the following command:

Bash

```
$ docker run -p 8080:8080 my-sklearn-app
```

This command will start a container from the my-sklearn-app image and map port 8080 on the host machine to port 8080 in the container. You can then access your application by navigating to http://localhost:8080 in your web browser.

Best Practices for Building Docker Images

Here are some tips for building efficient and secure Docker images for machine learning:

- Choose the right base image: Start with a minimal base image that contains only the necessary components. This helps to reduce image size and improve security.
- Use multi-stage builds: Multi-stage builds allow you to use separate images for building and running your application. This can help to reduce the size of the final image by discarding unnecessary build tools and dependencies.
- Optimize for layer caching: Structure your Dockerfile to take advantage of Docker's layer caching. Place frequently changing files lower in the Dockerfile to minimize rebuild times.
- Scan for vulnerabilities: Use tools like Snyk or Clair to scan your images for known vulnerabilities and keep them secure.
- Use a .dockerignore file: Create a .dockerignore file to exclude unnecessary files and directories from your image. This helps to reduce image size and improve build times.

Real-World Examples

- DataRobot: DataRobot, a leading automated machine learning platform, uses Docker to containerize its machine learning models and deploy them to various environments, including on-premises servers, cloud platforms, and edge devices.
- NVIDIA: NVIDIA uses Docker to package its deep learning software and GPU drivers, making it easier for developers to build and deploy GPU-accelerated applications.
- Tesla: Tesla uses Docker to deploy its machine learning models for autonomous driving, ensuring consistency and reliability across its fleet of vehicles.

Mastering the art of building Docker images, you're well on your way to creating portable, reproducible, and efficient machine learning deployments. In the next section, we'll discuss how to package your trained models and dependencies effectively.

3.3 Packaging ML Models and Dependencies

In the context of Docker and machine learning, this means making sure your Docker image contains everything your application needs to run, including:

- The trained model itself: This might be a file containing the model's architecture and weights (e.g., a .pkl file for a scikit-learn model, a .h5 file for a Keras model, or a saved model directory for a TensorFlow model).
- Required libraries and frameworks: Your application likely depends on specific versions of libraries like NumPy, Pandas, Scikit-learn, TensorFlow, or PyTorch. These need to be included in the image.
- Other dependencies: Any other files or assets your application needs, such as configuration files, data files, or auxiliary scripts.

Methods for Packaging Your Model

There are several ways to package your trained machine learning model within your Docker image. Let's explore the most common ones:

1. Directly Include the Model File

The simplest approach is to directly copy your trained model file into the Docker image during the build process.

Example:

```
Dockerfile

# ... other Dockerfile instructions ...

COPY model.pkl /app/model.pkl

# ... remaining Dockerfile instructions ...
```

This line in your Dockerfile copies the model.pkl file from your local directory into the /app directory within the container image.

Pros:

- Simple and straightforward.
- No external dependencies.

Cons:

- Can increase the image size, especially for large models.
- Makes it harder to update the model independently of the application code.

2. Use a Model Registry

A model registry is a centralized repository for storing and managing machine learning models. It provides versioning, access control, and other features that make it easier to manage your models throughout their lifecycle.

Popular model registries include:

- **MLflow Model Registry:** An open-source platform for managing the ML lifecycle, including model versioning, deployment, and monitoring.
- **TensorFlow Hub:** A repository of pre-trained TensorFlow models that can be easily reused and integrated into your applications.

- **AWS SageMaker Model Registry:** A fully managed service from AWS for storing, versioning, and deploying machine learning models.

Example (using MLflow):

```python
# In your training code:

import mlflow

# ... train your model ...

# Log the model to MLflow

mlflow.sklearn.log_model(model, "my-model")

# In your application code:

import mlflow

model_uri = "models:/my-model/latest"

loaded_model = mlflow.sklearn.load_model(model_uri)
```

In your Dockerfile, you would install the mlflow library and configure your application to load the model from the specified URI.

Pros:

- Centralized model management.
- Versioning and access control.
- Easier to update models independently.

Cons:

- Requires setting up and maintaining a model registry.

- Adds a dependency on the model registry.

3. Download from Cloud Storage

You can store your trained model in a cloud storage service like Amazon S3, Google Cloud Storage, or Azure Blob Storage. Your application can then download the model from the cloud at runtime.

Example:

Python

```python
# In your application code:

import boto3

s3 = boto3.client('s3')

s3.download_file('my-bucket', 'model.pkl', '/app/model.pkl')
```

Pros:

- Can handle very large models.
- Separates model storage from the application image.

Cons:

- Adds a dependency on the cloud storage service.
- Requires network connectivity to download the model.

The best approach for packaging your model will depend on factors like:

- Model size: For very large models, storing them in cloud storage might be more efficient.
- Update frequency: If you need to update your model frequently, using a model registry can simplify the process.

- Security requirements: If you have strict security requirements, using a model registry with access control might be necessary.
- Complexity: For simple applications, directly including the model file in the image might be sufficient.

Real-World Examples

- Netflix: Netflix uses a combination of model registries and cloud storage to manage its vast collection of machine learning models.
- Uber: Uber leverages a custom-built model registry to manage and deploy its machine learning models across its various services.
- Wayfair: Wayfair uses cloud storage to store its large image recognition models and downloads them to its application containers at runtime.

Carefully considering these options and choosing the right approach for your needs, you can effectively package your machine learning models and dependencies, ensuring your applications are ready for deployment on Kubernetes.

3.4 Optimizing Docker Images for Size and Performance

In the area of Docker, this means creating images that are as small and efficient as possible. Why is this important?

- Faster builds: Smaller images build faster, which speeds up your development cycle and allows you to iterate more quickly.
- Reduced storage costs: Smaller images take up less storage space, which can save you money, especially when storing many images in a registry.

- Improved network performance: Smaller images are faster to transfer over the network, which means faster deployments and updates.
- Enhanced security: Smaller images generally have a smaller attack surface, reducing the risk of vulnerabilities.

Techniques for Optimizing Docker Images

Let's explore some effective techniques for slimming down your Docker images and boosting their performance:

1. Choose a Minimal Base Image

Your Docker image starts with a base image, which provides the operating system and basic tools. Choosing a minimal base image is the first step towards optimization.

Instead of using a full-fledged operating system image like `ubuntu:latest`, consider using a slimmed-down version like `ubuntu:latest-slim` or a distroless image. These images contain only the essential components, resulting in significantly smaller image sizes.

For Python applications, consider using the `python:3.9-slim` image instead of the full `python:3.9` image.

2. Remove Unnecessary Files

Your Docker image should contain only the essential files needed to run your application. Avoid including unnecessary files like:

- Build tools: If you're using a compiled language like C++ or Java, you don't need to include the compiler and build tools in the final image.
- Test data: Remove any test data or sample files that are not required for your application to run.
- Development tools: Don't include development tools like debuggers or IDEs in the production image.

You can use a .dockerignore file to specify files and directories that should be excluded from the image.

3. Use Multi-Stage Builds

Multi-stage builds allow you to use multiple FROM instructions in your Dockerfile. This enables you to use a separate image for building your application and then copy only the necessary artifacts to a smaller final image.

Example:

```
Dockerfile

# Stage 1: Build the application

FROM python:3.9 AS builder

WORKDIR /app

COPY requirements.txt .

RUN pip install -r requirements.txt

COPY[1] . .

RUN python setup.py install

# Stage 2: Create the final image

FROM python:3.9-slim

WORKDIR /app

COPY --from=builder /app/dist/my-app .

CMD ["my-app"]
```

In this example, we use a builder stage to build our application. Then, we create a final image based on the slim Python image and copy only the built artifacts from the builder stage. This eliminates the need to include build tools and dependencies in the final image.

4. Optimize Layer Caching

Docker builds images in layers. Each instruction in your Dockerfile creates a new layer. Docker caches these layers to speed up subsequent builds.

To optimize layer caching, structure your Dockerfile so that frequently changing files are added later in the file. This way, when you make changes to your code, Docker can reuse the cached layers for the earlier instructions.

Example:

```
Dockerfile

# ... other instructions ...
COPY requirements.txt .
RUN pip install -r requirements.txt
COPY . . # Place this instruction later to avoid invalidating the cache
# ... other instructions ...
```

5. Use a Smaller Linux Distribution

If you're using a full Linux distribution as your base image, consider using a smaller distribution like Alpine Linux. Alpine Linux is designed to be small and secure, making it a good choice for containerized applications.

6. Compress Your Layers

You can use compression algorithms like gzip to compress the layers in your Docker image. This can significantly reduce the image size, especially for images with large text files or data.

Real-World Examples

- Pinterest: Pinterest reduced the size of its Docker images by 75% by implementing various optimization techniques, including multi-stage builds and layer caching. This resulted in faster builds, reduced storage costs, and improved performance.
- Spotify: Spotify optimized its Docker images by using a minimal base image, removing unnecessary files, and using multi-stage builds. This helped them to reduce image size and improve deployment times.
- Uber: Uber uses a combination of techniques, including multi-stage builds, layer caching, and compression, to optimize its Docker images for its microservices architecture.

By applying these optimization techniques, you can create Docker images that are lean, mean, and ready to race in your Kubernetes cluster. In the next section, we'll discuss security considerations for your containerized machine learning applications.

3.5 Security Considerations for Containerized ML Applications

We've built our efficient Docker images and are almost ready to deploy. But before we do, let's talk about security. Think of it like securing your home – you wouldn't leave the doors and windows wide open, right? You'd install locks, maybe an alarm system, and take precautions to protect your valuables.

Similarly, securing your containerized machine learning applications is crucial. It's about protecting your valuable data, models, and intellectual property from unauthorized access and malicious attacks.

Machine learning applications often deal with sensitive data, such as personal information, financial records, or medical records.

They also often involve complex dependencies and configurations, which can introduce vulnerabilities if not managed carefully.

Key Security Considerations

Let's explore some essential security practices for your containerized ML applications:

1. Choose a Trusted Base Image

Your Docker image starts with a base image. It's crucial to choose a base image from a trusted source, such as the official images on Docker Hub. These images are regularly updated with security patches and are less likely to contain vulnerabilities.

Avoid using unofficial or unmaintained images, as they might contain malware or outdated software.

2. Scan Your Images for Vulnerabilities

Even trusted base images can sometimes have vulnerabilities. It's a good practice to regularly scan your images for known vulnerabilities using tools like:

- Snyk: A comprehensive security platform that can scan your Docker images, code repositories, and other assets for vulnerabilities.
- Clair: An open-source static analysis tool that identifies vulnerabilities in Docker images.
- Anchor Engine: Another open-source platform for deep image inspection and vulnerability scanning.

These tools can help you identify and address potential security risks before they become a problem.

3. Minimize the Attack Surface

The attack surface refers to the points where an attacker can potentially access or exploit your application. To minimize the attack surface:

- Only include essential packages: Don't install unnecessary packages or dependencies in your image. Each additional package increases the potential for vulnerabilities.
- Remove unnecessary tools: Avoid including development tools, debugging tools, or other unnecessary software in your production images.
- Keep your images up-to-date: Regularly update your base images and application dependencies to patch security vulnerabilities.

4. Run Containers with Minimal Privileges

By default, Docker containers run as root. This gives them full access to the host system, which can be a security risk.

It's best practice to run your containers with a non-root user. This limits the container's privileges and reduces the potential damage if the container is compromised.

You can specify a user in your Dockerfile using the `USER` instruction.

5. Secure Your Secrets

Never store sensitive information, such as API keys, database credentials, or passwords, directly in your Docker image or application code. These secrets could be exposed if the image is compromised.

Instead, use Kubernetes secrets or other secure mechanisms to manage your secrets. Kubernetes secrets are encrypted at rest and can be securely mounted into your containers at runtime.

6. Network Security

Pay attention to network security within your Kubernetes cluster:

- Use network policies: Network policies allow you to control network traffic between pods in your cluster. This helps to prevent unauthorized access to your applications.
- Secure your ingress: Ingress is the entry point for external traffic to your cluster. Make sure your ingress controller is properly configured and secured.
- Use TLS encryption: Encrypt communication between your applications and services using TLS to protect data in transit.

Real-World Examples

- Capital One: Capital One, a major financial institution, uses Docker and Kubernetes to run its applications in a secure and compliant manner. They leverage security tools and best practices to protect their sensitive financial data.
- Tencent: Tencent, a leading technology company, uses Docker and Kubernetes to deploy its machine learning models for various applications, including image recognition, natural language processing, and fraud detection. They prioritize security by implementing strict access controls and vulnerability scanning.
- NASA: NASA uses Docker and Kubernetes to manage its scientific computing workloads, including simulations and data analysis. They adhere to strict security standards to protect their sensitive research data.

Security is an ongoing process. It's important to stay vigilant and keep up-to-date with the latest security best practices and vulnerabilities. Regularly review your Docker images and Kubernetes configurations to ensure they are secure.

By incorporating these security considerations into your containerized machine learning applications, you can protect your valuable assets and build a robust and secure foundation for your deployments.

Chapter 4: Building Machine Learning Workflows

In machine learning, this means managing the flow of data through various stages, from data ingestion and preprocessing to model training, evaluation, and deployment. Kubernetes, with its powerful orchestration capabilities, provides the perfect platform for building and managing these intricate workflows.

4.1 Orchestrating Data Pipelines

Let's talk about data pipelines! They're the lifeblood of any machine learning project, responsible for transforming raw data into valuable insights. Think of a data pipeline like an assembly line in a factory. Raw materials (data) enter the pipeline, go through various stages of processing and refinement, and emerge as finished products (trained models or valuable predictions).

In the world of machine learning, these pipelines can be quite complex, involving multiple steps like:

- Data Ingestion: Collecting data from various sources, such as databases, APIs, and streaming platforms.
- Data Validation and Cleaning: Ensuring data quality by checking for errors, inconsistencies, and missing values.
- Data Transformation: Converting data into a suitable format for model training, such as feature scaling, encoding categorical variables, and creating new features.
- Model Training: Training a machine learning model on the prepared data.
- Model Evaluation: Assessing the performance of the trained model.
- Model Deployment: Deploying the model for inference.

Orchestrating these pipelines effectively is crucial for ensuring efficiency, reproducibility, and scalability. This is where Kubernetes comes in, providing a robust platform for managing and executing complex data pipelines.

Two powerful tools that shine in this area are Argo and Kubeflow

Argo

Argo is an open-source container-native workflow engine for Kubernetes. It allows you to define your data pipeline as a Directed Acyclic Graph (DAG), where each node in the graph represents a step in your pipeline. Argo then takes care of executing these steps in the correct order, managing dependencies between steps, and handling failures gracefully.

Key Features of Argo for Data Pipelines

- DAG-based workflows: Define complex pipelines with dependencies and conditional execution. This allows you to create pipelines that branch based on conditions or run steps in parallel for improved efficiency.
- Artifact management: Argo can track and manage the inputs and outputs of each step in your pipeline. This ensures data lineage and reproducibility.
- Container-native execution: Each step in your pipeline is executed as a container, ensuring consistency and portability across different environments.
- Scalability and fault tolerance: Argo can handle large-scale pipelines with many steps and large datasets. It also provides mechanisms for automatic recovery from failures, ensuring your pipeline continues to run smoothly.
- Extensibility: Argo can be extended with plugins and custom steps to integrate with various tools and services.

Example Argo Workflow for Data Processing

Let's say you have a data pipeline that involves downloading data from an S3 bucket, preprocessing it, and then training a machine learning model. Here's how you might define this workflow in Argo:

YAML

```
apiVersion: argoproj.io/v1alpha1
kind: Workflow
metadata:
  generateName: data-pipeline-
spec:
  entrypoint: preprocess-train
  templates:
  - name: preprocess-train
    steps:
    - - name: download-data
        template: download-from-s3
    - - name: preprocess-data
        template: preprocess
      - name: train-model
        template: train
  - name: download-from-s3
    container:
      image: my-s3-downloader:latest
      command: ["python", "download.py"]
      args: ["{{workflow.parameters.s3_bucket}}", "{{workflow.parameters.s3_key}}"]
  - name: preprocess
```

```
    container:
      image: my-preprocessing-image:latest
      command: ["python", "preprocess.py"]
  - name: train
    container:
      image: my-training-image:latest
      command: ["python", "train.py"]
```

In this example, we define a workflow with three steps: download-data, preprocess-data, and train-model. Each step is defined as a template that specifies the container image to use and the command to execute. The workflow parameters allow you to customize the S3 bucket and key for data download.

Kubeflow

Kubeflow is an open-source platform specifically designed for machine learning on Kubernetes. It provides a comprehensive suite of tools and components for building, training, tuning, and deploying machine learning models.

Key Features of Kubeflow for Data Pipelines

- Kubeflow Pipelines: This component allows you to define and execute portable and scalable machine learning pipelines. You can define your pipeline using a Python SDK or a visual editor, and Kubeflow Pipelines takes care of orchestrating the execution on your Kubernetes cluster.
- Jupyter Notebooks: Kubeflow provides a Jupyter notebook server for interactive development and experimentation. You can use notebooks to explore your data, develop your models, and build your pipelines.
- Katib: This component provides automated hyperparameter tuning and model selection capabilities. You can define a search space for your hyperparameters, and Katib will

automatically explore this space to find the optimal configuration.
- KFServing: This component simplifies the deployment and serving of machine learning models. It provides a serverless framework for deploying models as scalable APIs.

Example Kubeflow Pipeline

Let's say you want to build a pipeline that preprocesses data, trains a model, and then evaluates its performance. Here's how you might define this pipeline using the Kubeflow Pipelines SDK:

Python

```python
import kfp
from kfp import dsl
@dsl.pipeline(
    name='my-pipeline',
    description='A simple machine learning pipeline'
)
def my_pipeline(data_path: str):
    preprocess_op = dsl.ContainerOp(
        name='preprocess',
        image='my-preprocessing-image:latest',
        arguments=[
            '--data-path', data_path
        ]
    )
    train_op = dsl.ContainerOp(
        name='train',
```

```
        image='my-training-image:latest',
        arguments=[
            '--input-data', preprocess_op.output
        ]
    )
    evaluate_op = dsl.ContainerOp(
        name='evaluate',
        image='my-evaluation-image:latest',
        arguments=[
            '--model-path', train_op.output
        ]
    )
```

In this example, we define a pipeline with three steps: preprocess, train, and evaluate. Each step is defined as a ContainerOp, which specifies the container image to use and the arguments to pass. The dsl.pipeline decorator defines the pipeline's metadata and parameters.

Both Argo and Kubeflow are powerful tools for orchestrating data pipelines on Kubernetes. The best choice for you will depend on your specific needs and preferences.

- Argo: A good choice if you need a general-purpose workflow engine for Kubernetes and want fine-grained control over your pipeline execution.
- Kubeflow: A good choice if you're specifically focused on machine learning and want a platform with built-in tools for model training, hyperparameter tuning, and deployment.

Real-World Examples

- Spotify: Spotify uses Kubeflow to manage its machine learning pipelines for music recommendation and personalization.
- Bloomberg: Bloomberg uses Argo to orchestrate its data pipelines for financial data processing and analysis.
- CERN: CERN uses Kubeflow to manage its machine learning workflows for high-energy physics research.

Leveraging these tools, you can effectively orchestrate your data pipelines on Kubernetes, ensuring efficiency, scalability, and reproducibility in your machine learning projects.

4.2 Running Distributed Training Jobs

In machine learning, this means splitting your training workload across multiple machines (or worker nodes) in your Kubernetes cluster. This can significantly reduce training time, especially for large datasets and complex models.

Kubernetes provides the perfect platform for running distributed training jobs. It handles the complexities of managing the worker nodes, distributing the data, and coordinating the training process.

Why Distribute Training?

- Faster training: Distributing the workload across multiple machines can significantly reduce training time, allowing you to iterate faster and experiment with more models.
- Larger datasets: You can train on larger datasets that might not fit on a single machine.
- More complex models: You can train more complex models that require more computational resources.

Distributed Training with TensorFlow

TensorFlow, a popular open-source machine learning framework, offers excellent support for distributed training. It provides a tf.distribute.Strategy API that allows you to distribute your training workload across multiple workers with minimal code changes.

Here's a simplified example of how to use tf.distribute.Strategy with Kubernetes:

```python
import tensorflow as tf

# Define your model
model = tf.keras.models.Sequential([
    # ... your model layers ...
])

# Define your distributed strategy
strategy = tf.distribute.MirroredStrategy()

# Define your training step
@tf.function
def train_step(images, labels):
    with strategy.scope():
        # ... your training logic ...

# Distribute the dataset
dataset = ...  # your dataset
dist_dataset = strategy.experimental_distribute_dataset(dataset)

# Train the model
```

```
for epoch in range(epochs):

    for images, labels in dist_dataset:

        train_step(images, labels)
```

In this example, we use the MirroredStrategy to distribute the training across multiple GPUs on different worker nodes. The strategy.scope() ensures that the model variables are mirrored across all workers.

To run this code on Kubernetes, you would package it into a Docker image and create a Kubernetes Job that specifies the number of worker pods and their resource requirements.

Distributed Training with PyTorch

PyTorch, another popular machine learning framework, also provides robust support for distributed training. It uses the torch.distributed package to enable communication and coordination between worker processes.

Here's a simplified example of how to use torch.distributed with Kubernetes:

Python

```python
import torch

import torch.distributed as dist

# Initialize the distributed process group

dist.init_process_group(backend='nccl')

# Define your model

model = ... # your model
```

```
# Distribute the model
model =
torch.nn.parallel.DistributedDataParallel(model)

# Define your training step
def train_step(images, labels):
  # ... your training logic ...

# Train the model
for epoch in range(epochs):
  for images, labels in train_loader:
    train_step(images, labels)
```

In this example, we use the nccl backend for efficient communication between GPUs on different nodes. The DistributedDataParallel wrapper distributes the model and data across the workers.

To run this code on Kubernetes, you would package it into a Docker image and create a Kubernetes Job that specifies the number of worker pods and their resource requirements.

Key Considerations for Distributed Training

- Communication overhead: Communication between worker nodes can introduce overhead. Choose an efficient communication backend and optimize your code to minimize communication.
- Data parallelism vs. model parallelism: Data parallelism involves splitting the data across workers, while model parallelism involves splitting the model itself. Choose the approach that best suits your model and hardware.

- Fault tolerance: Ensure your training process can recover from worker failures. Kubernetes can automatically restart failed pods, but you might need to implement additional fault tolerance mechanisms in your code.

Real-World Examples

- OpenAI: OpenAI uses Kubernetes to train its large language models, such as GPT-3, on massive datasets using distributed training.
- Meta: Meta (formerly Facebook) uses Kubernetes to train its machine learning models for tasks like image recognition, natural language processing, and content recommendation.
- Tesla: Tesla uses Kubernetes to train its self-driving car models on vast amounts of driving data collected from its fleet of vehicles.

By leveraging Kubernetes and the distributed training capabilities of frameworks like TensorFlow and PyTorch, you can accelerate your model training and tackle even the most demanding machine learning challenges.

4.3 Hyperparameter Tuning and Model Selection

In machine learning, you need to find the optimal hyperparameters for your model. These are settings that control the learning process, such as the learning rate, batch size, number of layers in a neural network, or the number of trees in a random forest.

Finding the best hyperparameters can significantly impact your model's performance. But manually trying different combinations can be tedious and time-consuming. That's where hyperparameter tuning comes in.

Hyperparameter Tuning

Hyperparameter tuning is the process of systematically exploring different hyperparameter configurations to find the one that yields the best performance for your model. It's like conducting a series of experiments to discover the secret recipe for your machine learning model.

There are various techniques for hyperparameter tuning, including:

- Manual search: Manually trying different combinations of hyperparameters. This can be time-consuming and inefficient, especially for models with many hyperparameters.
- Grid search: Defining a grid of hyperparameter values and trying all possible combinations. This is more systematic than manual search but can still be computationally expensive.
- Random search: Randomly sampling hyperparameter values from a defined search space. This can be more efficient than grid search, especially for high-dimensional spaces.
- Bayesian optimization: Using a probabilistic model to guide the search for optimal hyperparameters. This can be more efficient than random search and often finds better solutions.

Kubernetes for Hyperparameter Tuning

Kubernetes can be a powerful tool for hyperparameter tuning. It allows you to run multiple training jobs in parallel, each with a different hyperparameter configuration. This can significantly speed up the tuning process.

Here's how you can use Kubernetes for hyperparameter tuning:

1. Define your hyperparameter search space: Specify the range of values for each hyperparameter you want to tune.
2. Create a training job for each configuration: Use Kubernetes Jobs to launch multiple training jobs, each with a different set of hyperparameters.
3. Monitor the jobs: Track the progress of each job and collect the evaluation metrics.
4. Analyze the results: Compare the performance of different hyperparameter configurations and select the best one.

Tools for Hyperparameter Tuning on Kubernetes

Several tools can help you automate hyperparameter tuning on Kubernetes:

- Kubeflow Katib: Katib is a component of Kubeflow that provides automated hyperparameter tuning and neural architecture search capabilities. It supports various search algorithms, including grid search, random search, and Bayesian optimization.
- Cloud-based hyperparameter tuning services: Cloud providers like Google Cloud, AWS, and Azure offer managed hyperparameter tuning services that integrate with Kubernetes. These services can simplify the tuning process and provide access to specialized hardware like GPUs and TPUs.

Model Selection

Model selection involves evaluating the performance of each model on a held-out dataset (the validation set) and choosing the model that performs best according to your chosen metrics.

Kubernetes can help you automate model selection by running evaluation jobs for each trained model and comparing their performance.

Key Considerations for Hyperparameter Tuning and Model Selection

- Evaluation metrics: Choose appropriate evaluation metrics that align with your business goals.
- Cross-validation: Use cross-validation techniques to get a more robust estimate of your model's performance.
- Computational resources: Hyperparameter tuning can be computationally expensive. Consider using cloud-based resources or specialized hardware to accelerate the process.
- Early stopping: Implement early stopping to terminate training jobs that are not showing improvement, saving time and resources.

Real-World Examples

- Netflix: Netflix uses hyperparameter tuning to optimize its recommendation models, improving the accuracy of its suggestions and enhancing user experience.
- Airbnb: Airbnb uses hyperparameter tuning to fine-tune its search ranking models, ensuring that users find the most relevant listings.
- Wayfair: Wayfair uses hyperparameter tuning and model selection to optimize its image recognition models, improving the accuracy of its product categorization and search results.

By effectively leveraging Kubernetes for hyperparameter tuning and model selection, you can unlock the full potential of your machine learning models and achieve optimal performance for your applications.

4.4 Managing Data and Model Versioning

Let's talk about version control! You know how important it is to keep track of changes to your code, right? You use Git or other version control systems to track revisions, collaborate with others, and revert to previous versions if needed.

Well, the same principle applies to your data and machine learning models. Think of it like keeping a detailed lab notebook where you meticulously record every experiment, every dataset used, and every model trained. This allows you to reproduce your results, track your progress, and collaborate effectively with others.

In the context of machine learning, versioning your data and models is crucial for:

- Reproducibility: Ensuring that you can recreate your experiments and results, which is essential for scientific rigor and debugging.
- Traceability: Understanding the lineage of your data and models, from the original source to the final deployed version.
- Collaboration: Enabling effective collaboration with others by providing a clear history of changes and allowing for easy sharing of data and models.
- Auditing and governance: Maintaining a record of your machine learning activities for compliance and auditing purposes.

Data Versioning

Data is the foundation of any machine learning project. It's essential to keep track of the different versions of your data, including:

- Raw data: The original data you collect from various sources.
- Processed data: The data after cleaning, transformation, and feature engineering.

- Training, validation, and test sets: The different splits of your data used for training, evaluating, and testing your models.

Tools for Data Versioning

Several tools can help you manage and version your data:

- DVC (Data Version Control): An open-source tool that allows you to version your datasets and track their lineage. It integrates with Git and cloud storage to provide a comprehensive solution for data management.
- Git Large File Storage (LFS): An extension to Git that allows you to store large files, such as datasets, outside of your main Git repository.
- Cloud storage versioning: Cloud storage services like Amazon S3, Google Cloud Storage, and Azure Blob Storage offer built-in versioning capabilities that allow you to keep track of different versions of your data.

Example using DVC:

```bash
# Initialize DVC in your project
$ dvc init

# Track a data file
$ dvc add data.csv

# Commit the changes to Git
$ git commit -m "Add data.csv"

# Push the data to remote storage
$ dvc push
```

Model Versioning

Just like your data, your machine learning models also need to be versioned. This allows you to:

- Track different versions of your model: As you experiment with different architectures, hyperparameters, and training data, you'll generate different versions of your model. Versioning allows you to keep track of these versions and their performance.
- Reproduce experiments: You can easily reproduce past experiments by loading a specific version of your model and data.
- Roll back to previous versions: If a new version of your model performs poorly, you can easily roll back to a previous version.
- Deploy specific versions: You can deploy specific versions of your model to different environments, such as staging or production.

Tools for Model Versioning

Several tools can help you manage and version your machine learning models:

- MLflow Model Registry: An open-source platform for managing the ML lifecycle, including model versioning, deployment, and monitoring.
- TensorFlow Hub: A repository of pre-trained TensorFlow models that can be easily reused and integrated into your applications.
- AWS SageMaker Model Registry: A fully managed service from AWS for storing, versioning, and deploying machine learning models.

Example using MLflow:

```python
# In your training code:

import mlflow

# ... train your model ...

# Log the model to MLflow

mlflow.sklearn.log_model(model, "my-model")

# Register the model in the Model Registry

model_uri = "runs:/{}/my-model".format(mlflow.active_run().info.run_id)

mv = mlflow.register_model(model_uri, "MyModel")
```

Integrating with Kubernetes

Kubernetes provides a natural platform for managing and deploying different versions of your models. You can use Kubernetes deployments to deploy specific versions of your model and use services to route traffic to the appropriate version.

Real-World Examples

- Netflix: Netflix uses a combination of model registries and cloud storage versioning to manage its vast collection of machine learning models.
- Uber: Uber leverages a custom-built model registry to manage and deploy its machine learning models across its various services.
- Wayfair: Wayfair uses a combination of DVC and cloud storage versioning to manage its datasets and model training artifacts.

By implementing robust data and model versioning practices, you can ensure reproducibility, traceability, and collaboration in your machine learning projects, laying the foundation for successful deployments on Kubernetes.

Chapter 5: Deploying Machine Learning Models

This chapter is all about deploying your model – making it accessible to users or other applications so it can do its magic. Think of it like opening a shop after stocking it with amazing products. You need to set up the storefront, arrange the displays, and let customers know you're open for business.

5.1 Deployment Patterns

You've put in the hard work, trained your machine learning model, and optimized it for peak performance. Now, it's time to share your creation with the world! This section explores how to deploy your model – making it accessible to users or other applications that need its predictions.

Think of it like choosing the right transportation method for your goods. Do you need a speedy courier service for urgent deliveries, a reliable cargo ship for bulk transport, or a scheduled train service for regular shipments? Similarly, different deployment patterns cater to different needs and scenarios in machine learning.

Let's explore the most common ways to deploy your model:

1. REST APIs

REST APIs (Representational State Transfer Application Programming Interfaces) are a popular way to deploy machine learning models as web services. This allows other applications or users to interact with your model through standard HTTP requests, just like they interact with any other website or web application.

How it Works

- **Packaging:** You package your trained model and a web server (like Flask or FastAPI in Python) into a Docker container. This container holds everything needed to run your model and serve predictions.
- **API Endpoint:** The web server exposes an API endpoint, which is like a specific URL that accepts requests. These requests typically include the input data for your model.
- **Prediction:** When a request arrives at the endpoint, the server preprocesses the input data, passes it to your model, obtains the prediction, and sends the result back in the response.

Example (using Flask):

Python

```python
from flask import Flask, request, jsonify
import pickle

app = Flask(__name__)

# Load your trained model
with open('model.pkl', 'rb') as f:
    model = pickle.load(f)

@app.route('/predict', methods=['POST'])
def predict():
    data = request.get_json()  # Get input data from the request

    # Preprocess the data (e.g., feature scaling, encoding)

    # ...
```

```
    prediction = model.predict(data)   # Get
prediction from the model

    # Postprocess the prediction (e.g., convert
to probabilities)

    # ...

    return jsonify({'prediction': prediction})   #
Return prediction as JSON

if __name__ == '__main__':

    app.run(debug=True, host='0.0.0.0')
```

This code snippet demonstrates a simple Flask application that loads a pre-trained model (model.pkl) and exposes a /predict endpoint. When a client sends a POST request with input data to this endpoint, the server uses the loaded model to generate a prediction and returns it as a JSON response.

Pros:

- Widely adopted: REST APIs are a standard way to build web services, making them easy to integrate with various applications and programming languages.
- Scalability: You can easily scale your REST API deployments using Kubernetes to handle increasing traffic and demand.
- Flexibility: REST APIs can handle various data formats (JSON, XML, etc.) and support different HTTP methods (GET, POST, PUT, DELETE) for different actions.

Cons:

- Overhead: For large or complex input data, the serialization and deserialization of data in REST APIs can add overhead.

- Efficiency: REST might not be the most efficient choice for high-performance scenarios or real-time applications with strict latency requirements.

2. gRPC

gRPC (Google Remote Procedure Call) is a modern, high-performance framework for building distributed applications and APIs. It uses Protocol Buffers (protobuf) for efficient data serialization and offers features like streaming and bidirectional communication.

Think of gRPC as a dedicated express lane for your model's predictions. It's designed for speed and efficiency, making it a good choice for applications that require low latency or handle large amounts of data.

How it Works

- Define the service: You define the interface for your machine learning service using protobuf, a language-agnostic mechanism for serializing structured data.
- Implement the service: You implement the service using gRPC libraries in your preferred programming language. This involves writing code to handle client requests, preprocess data, invoke your model, and return predictions.
- Packaging: You package your model and the gRPC server into a Docker container.
- Client interaction: Clients can then call your service methods using gRPC, benefiting from efficient communication and data transfer.

Pros:

- Performance: gRPC is generally more efficient than REST for large or complex data due to its use of protobuf for serialization.

- Streaming: gRPC supports streaming, which allows for efficient transfer of large datasets or real-time communication.
- Type safety: Protobuf enforces type checking, reducing the risk of errors due to data type mismatches.

Cons:

- Complexity: Setting up and using gRPC can be more complex than REST, especially for those unfamiliar with protobuf.
- Browser support: gRPC has limited direct support in web browsers, which might require using proxies or gateways for web-based clients.

3. Batch Predictions

Batch prediction is an offline approach where you process a batch of data and store the results for later retrieval. This is useful when you don't need real-time predictions and can process data in bulk.

How it Works

- Batch processing script: You write a script that loads your trained model and processes a batch of input data. This script might read data from a file, a database, or a message queue.
- Scheduling: You schedule this script to run periodically or trigger it based on events using tools like Kubernetes CronJobs.
- Storage: The predictions generated by your script are stored in a database, a data warehouse, or a cloud storage service.
- Access: Applications or users can then access the pre-computed predictions as needed.

Pros:

- Efficiency: Batch prediction is very efficient for processing large datasets, as it can leverage distributed computing and optimized data processing techniques.
- Cost-effectiveness: You can schedule batch jobs to run during off-peak hours when computing resources are cheaper.
- Reduced load: Batch predictions can reduce the load on your real-time prediction systems by pre-computing results for common queries.

Cons:

- Latency: Not suitable for real-time applications that require immediate predictions.
- Staleness: Predictions might become stale if the underlying data or model changes frequently.

Choosing the Right Deployment Pattern

The best deployment pattern for your machine learning model depends on several factors:

- Real-time requirements: If you need real-time predictions, REST APIs or gRPC are suitable choices.
- Data volume and complexity: For large or complex data, gRPC or batch predictions might be more efficient.
- Client requirements: Consider the needs of your clients and their preferred ways to interact with your model.
- Infrastructure: Choose a pattern that aligns with your infrastructure and deployment environment.

By carefully considering these factors, you can choose the most effective deployment pattern for your machine learning model and ensure it meets the needs of your users or applications.

5.2 Exposing Models with Kubernetes Services and Ingress

A Kubernetes Service is an abstraction that defines a logical set of pods and a policy by which to access them. It provides a stable network endpoint for accessing your application, regardless of how many pods are running or where they are located in the cluster.

Think of a Service as the internal phone operator within your company. When someone calls the main company number, the operator directs the call to the appropriate department or employee. Similarly, a Service directs traffic to the correct pods running your application.

Key benefits of Services:

- Stable endpoint: Services provide a consistent IP address and port that clients can use to access your application, even if the underlying pods are moved or replaced.
- Load balancing: Services can distribute traffic across multiple pods, ensuring high availability and fault tolerance.
- Service discovery: Services make it easy for applications within the cluster to find and communicate with each other.

Types of Services

Kubernetes offers different types of Services, each suited for different scenarios:

- ClusterIP: This is the default type. It exposes the Service on a cluster-internal IP. This means your application can be accessed by other applications within the cluster but not from outside.
- NodePort: This exposes the Service on each node's IP at a static port. This allows external access to your application, but it might not be the most efficient or secure option.

- LoadBalancer: This exposes the Service externally using a cloud provider's load balancer. This is a common way to expose applications to the internet.
- ExternalName: This maps the Service to an external DNS name.

Example Service Definition

YAML

```yaml
apiVersion: v1
kind: Service
metadata:
  name: my-ml-service
spec:
  selector:
    app: my-ml-app  # This should match the label of your Deployment
  ports:
  - protocol: TCP
    port: 80  # The port exposed by the Service
    targetPort: 8080  # The port your application listens on
  type: LoadBalancer  # Expose the Service externally
```

Kubernetes Ingress

While Services provide internal access and basic external access, Ingress takes it a step further. It acts as a sophisticated gateway that manages external access to services in your cluster, typically via HTTP.

Think of Ingress as the receptionist at your company's front desk. They greet visitors, direct them to the appropriate department, and handle incoming mail. Similarly, Ingress routes incoming HTTP traffic to the correct services based on rules you define.

Key benefits of Ingress:

- Simplified routing: You can define rules to route traffic to different services based on the request's host, path, or headers.
- TLS termination: Ingress can handle TLS encryption, offloading the burden from your application.
- Centralized configuration: You can manage all your external access rules in one place.

Example Ingress Definition

```yaml
YAML

apiVersion: networking.k8s.io/v1

kind: Ingress

metadata:
  name: my-ml-ingress

spec:
  rules:
  - host: my-ml-app.example.com
```

```
      http:
        paths:
        - path: /predict
          pathType: Prefix
          backend:
            service:
              name: my-ml-service
              port:
                number: 80
```

This Ingress definition routes all traffic to my-ml-app.example.com/predict to the my-ml-service Service.

Putting it Together

1. Deploy your model: Package your model and web server into a Docker container and deploy it using a Kubernetes Deployment.
2. Create a Service: Create a Service to expose your model internally within the cluster.
3. Create an Ingress: If you need external access, create an Ingress resource to define the routing rules for your application.

Real-World Examples

- Airbnb: Airbnb uses Ingress to route traffic to its various microservices, including its machine learning models for search ranking and fraud detection.

- Pinterest: Pinterest uses Ingress to manage external access to its image recognition and recommendation services, ensuring high availability and security.
- Spotify: Spotify uses Ingress to route traffic to its music streaming and personalization services, handling millions of requests per second.

Effectively using Kubernetes Services and Ingress, you can expose your machine learning models to the world, making them accessible and ready to provide valuable predictions.

5.3 A/B Testing and Canary Deployments for ML

You've deployed your machine learning model, and it's serving predictions. But the journey doesn't stop there! Just like any software application, your model needs to evolve and improve over time. You might want to experiment with new algorithms, features, or hyperparameters to boost its performance.

But how do you introduce these changes safely without disrupting your users or causing unexpected issues? That's where A/B testing and canary deployments come in. These techniques allow you to test new versions of your model in a controlled manner, gradually rolling them out and monitoring their performance before making them available to everyone.

Think of it like testing a new recipe in your restaurant. You wouldn't immediately replace your signature dish with a completely new one, right? You might first offer it as a special to a small group of customers to get their feedback and see how it performs.

A/B Testing

A/B testing involves deploying two or more versions of your model (A and B) simultaneously and directing a portion of your traffic to each version. You then monitor the performance of each version, comparing metrics like accuracy, latency, and user engagement to determine which one performs better.

This allows you to experiment with different approaches and gather data on their effectiveness before committing to a particular version.

How to Implement A/B Testing with Kubernetes

1. Deploy multiple versions: Create separate Kubernetes Deployments for each version of your model. Each Deployment will have its own unique label (e.g., version=A and version=B).
2. Create Services: Create separate Kubernetes Services for each version, targeting the corresponding Deployments.
3. Configure Ingress: Use an Ingress resource to route traffic to different Services based on rules you define. You can use annotations or custom resource definitions to configure the Ingress to split traffic between the versions. For example, you might route 50% of traffic to version A and 50% to version B.
4. Monitor and analyze: Monitor the performance of each version using metrics and logs. Analyze the results to determine which version performs better according to your chosen criteria.

Example Ingress with A/B Testing

```yaml
apiVersion: networking.k8s.io/v1

kind: Ingress

metadata:
  name: my-ml-ingress
```

```yaml
  annotations:
    nginx.ingress.kubernetes.io/ab-testing: "true"
    nginx.ingress.kubernetes.io/ab-testing-splitting-type: "percentage"
    nginx.ingress.kubernetes.io/ab-testing-cookie-name: "my-ab-cookie"
spec:
  rules:
  - host: my-ml-app.example.com
    http:
      paths:
      - path: /predict
        pathType: Prefix
        backend:
          service:
            name: my-ml-service-a
            port:
              number: 80
      - path: /predict
        pathType: Prefix
```

```
      backend:
        service:
          name: my-ml-service-b
          port:
            number: 80
```

This Ingress configuration uses annotations to enable A/B testing with a 50/50 traffic split between my-ml-service-a and my-ml-service-b.

Canary Deployments

Canary deployments involve gradually rolling out a new version of your model to a small subset of users or traffic. You monitor the performance of the new version and gradually increase the traffic to it if it performs well.

This allows you to catch any issues or regressions with the new version before it impacts a large portion of your user base.

How to Implement Canary Deployments with Kubernetes

1. **Deploy the new version:** Create a new Kubernetes Deployment for the new version of your model.
2. **Update the Service:** Update your Service to include the new Deployment, but initially route only a small percentage of traffic to it.
3. **Monitor and analyze:** Monitor the performance of the new version using metrics and logs.
4. **Gradually increase traffic:** If the new version performs well, gradually increase the traffic routed to it until it handles all the traffic.

Example Service with Canary Deployment

YAML

```yaml
apiVersion: v1
kind: Service
metadata:
  name: my-ml-service
spec:
  selector:
    app: my-ml-app
  ports:
  - protocol: TCP
    port: 80
    targetPort: 8080
  type: LoadBalancer
```

To implement a canary deployment, you could initially create two Deployments, one with app: my-ml-app, version: v1 and another with app: my-ml-app, version: v2. The Service, as defined above, would select pods with the label app: my-ml-app, which includes both versions. Then, you can utilize a service mesh like Istio or Linkerd to control traffic splitting between v1 and v2 pods.

Benefits of A/B Testing and Canary Deployments

- Reduced risk: By gradually rolling out new versions, you reduce the risk of widespread issues or regressions.

- Improved user experience: You can ensure that new versions of your model perform well before they are exposed to all users.
- Data-driven decisions: You can make data-driven decisions about which model version to use based on its performance.
- Faster iteration: You can experiment with new ideas and get feedback quickly.

Real-World Examples

- **Netflix:** Netflix uses A/B testing extensively to experiment with different recommendation algorithms and user interface designs.
- **Facebook:** Facebook uses canary deployments to roll out new features and updates to its massive user base.
- **Uber:** Uber uses A/B testing and canary deployments to optimize its pricing models and ensure a smooth user experience.

Incorporating A/B testing and canary deployments into your machine learning deployment strategy, you can confidently introduce new models and updates, ensuring a smooth and reliable experience for your users.

5.4 Monitoring Model Performance and Health

You've successfully deployed your machine learning model and it's out there making predictions. But your job isn't done yet. Think of it like launching a satellite into space. You wouldn't just launch it and forget about it, right? You'd constantly monitor its trajectory, its systems, and its environment to ensure it's functioning correctly and achieving its mission.

Similarly, monitoring your deployed machine learning model is crucial for ensuring its continued success. It's about keeping a close eye on its performance, health, and overall behavior to detect any issues, maintain quality of service, and gain insights for improvement.

Why Monitor Your Model?

- Detecting and diagnosing issues: Things can go wrong in production. Your model might encounter unexpected data, experience performance degradation, or suffer from resource constraints. Monitoring helps you identify these issues quickly and diagnose their root cause.
- Ensure quality of service: Your model needs to meet certain performance expectations, such as accuracy, latency, and throughput. Monitoring helps you track these metrics and ensure your model is delivering the desired quality of service.
- Trigger alerts: You can set up alerts to notify you if any critical metrics deviate from the expected range. This allows you to take corrective action before problems escalate.
- Gain insights: Monitoring provides valuable insights into how your model is being used and how it behaves in the real world. This can help you identify areas for improvement, such as retraining your model with new data or optimizing its performance.

Key Metrics to Monitor

What should you monitor? Here are some essential metrics for your machine learning models:

- Accuracy, precision, recall, F1-score: These metrics measure the predictive performance of your model.
- Latency: The time it takes for your model to generate a prediction.
- Throughput: The number of predictions your model can generate per second.
- Resource utilization: The amount of CPU, memory, and other resources your model is consuming.

- Error rate: The number of errors or exceptions encountered by your model.
- Data drift: The degree to which the input data distribution changes over time.
- Model drift: The degradation of your model's performance over time due to changes in the data distribution or the environment.

Tools and Techniques for Monitoring

Kubernetes provides a rich ecosystem of tools and techniques for monitoring your deployed models:

- Logging: Collect logs from your application and model to track errors, warnings, and other events. You can use Kubernetes' built-in logging mechanisms or integrate with external logging services like Elasticsearch and Kibana.
- Metrics: Use tools like Prometheus to collect metrics from your application and model. Prometheus is an open-source monitoring system that can scrape metrics from your application endpoints and store them in a time-series database.
- Tracing: Use tools like Jaeger to trace requests through your application and model. Tracing helps you understand the flow of requests and identify performance bottlenecks.
- Health checks: Implement health checks in your application to ensure your model is responding correctly to requests. Kubernetes can periodically check the health of your pods and restart them if they fail.
- Dashboards: Use tools like Grafana to create dashboards that visualize your metrics and provide insights into your model's performance.

Example: Monitoring with Prometheus and Grafana

1. Instrument your application: Add code to your application to expose metrics using the Prometheus client library.

2. Deploy Prometheus: Deploy Prometheus to your Kubernetes cluster to scrape metrics from your application.
3. Deploy Grafana: Deploy Grafana to your cluster to create dashboards and visualize your metrics.
4. Create dashboards: Use Grafana's query language to create dashboards that display key metrics like accuracy, latency, and throughput.

Real-World Examples

- Netflix: Netflix uses a sophisticated monitoring system to track the performance of its recommendation models and ensure a seamless user experience.
- Uber: Uber monitors its machine learning models for fraud detection and ETA prediction to ensure accuracy and reliability.
- Airbnb: Airbnb uses monitoring tools to track the performance of its search ranking and pricing models, ensuring they meet business goals.

Monitoring is not just about detecting problems; it's also about continuous improvement. By analyzing your monitoring data, you can gain valuable insights into your model's behavior and identify opportunities to enhance its performance, efficiency, and reliability.

By incorporating comprehensive monitoring into your machine learning deployment strategy, you can ensure your models continue to deliver value and meet the evolving needs of your users or applications.

Chapter 6: Scaling and Resource Management

Your machine learning model is deployed and serves predictions. But as your user base grows and your application becomes more popular, you'll need to ensure it can handle the increasing demand. Think of it like a growing plant – it needs more space, water, and nutrients to thrive as it gets bigger.

Similarly, your machine learning application needs more resources to handle increased traffic and workload. This chapter is all about scaling your application and managing its resources effectively on Kubernetes. We'll explore how to allocate resources efficiently, scale your application automatically, and optimize for cost and performance.

6.1 Understanding Resource Requests and Limits

Just like you need food and water to function, your applications need resources like CPU, memory, and sometimes GPUs to run properly. In Kubernetes, you can precisely control how these resources are allocated to your containers using resource requests and limits.

Think of it like ordering a meal at a restaurant. You might request a specific dish (resource request), and the restaurant will ensure it's prepared for you. You might also specify any dietary restrictions or preferences (resource limits) to ensure the meal meets your needs.

Similarly, resource requests and limits in Kubernetes allow you to define the resource requirements of your containers, ensuring they get the necessary resources while preventing them from consuming too much and impacting other applications.

Resource Requests

Resource requests are what your container asks for from the Kubernetes scheduler. It's like telling the scheduler, "I need at least this much CPU and memory to function properly."

- CPU requests: Specify the amount of CPU cores your container needs. You can use units like millicores (e.g., 100m for 100 millicores, which is 0.1 CPU).
- Memory requests: Specify the amount of memory your container needs. You can use units like bytes, kilobytes, megabytes, or gigabytes (e.g., 1Gi for 1 gigabyte).

Kubernetes uses these requests to schedule your pods onto nodes with sufficient capacity. If a node doesn't have enough available resources to meet the requests of a pod, the pod won't be scheduled on that node.

Resource Limits

Resource limits are the maximum amount of resources a container is allowed to consume. It's like setting a budget for your meal – you don't want to overspend, even if the restaurant offers extra-large portions.

- CPU limits: Specify the maximum amount of CPU cores your container can use.
- Memory limits: Specify the maximum amount of memory your container can use.

Limits prevent a container from using more resources than it's allowed, even if those resources are available on the node. This prevents one application from hogging resources and starving others.

Example:

YAML

```yaml
apiVersion: v1
kind: Pod
metadata:
  name: my-ml-pod
spec:
  containers:
  - name: my-ml-container
    image: my-ml-image:latest
    resources:
      requests:
        cpu: 100m
        memory: 256Mi
      limits:
        cpu: 500m
        memory: 1Gi
```

In this example, the container requests 100 millicores of CPU and 256 megabytes of memory. It can use up to 500 milli cores of CPU and 1 gigabyte of memory, but no more.

Why are Requests and Limits Important?

- Scheduling: Kubernetes uses resource requests to make intelligent scheduling decisions. It ensures that pods are placed on nodes with enough resources to meet their needs.
- Resource Allocation: Limits prevent resource contention and ensure fair allocation across different applications. This

prevents one application from monopolizing resources and impacting the performance of others.
- Quality of Service: Properly configured requests and limits can help guarantee your application's performance and stability. If your application needs a certain amount of resources to function correctly, setting appropriate requests ensures it gets those resources.

Best Practices for Setting Requests and Limits

- Start with requests: It's generally recommended to start by setting resource requests. This helps Kubernetes schedule your pods effectively.
- Monitor your application: Monitor your application's resource usage to understand its actual needs. You can use tools like Kubernetes' built-in monitoring or external monitoring systems like Prometheus and Grafana.
- Adjust as needed: Based on your monitoring data, adjust your requests and limits to optimize resource allocation and performance.
- Don't over-request or over-limit: Over-requesting resources can lead to inefficient resource utilization, while over-limiting can cause your application to crash or perform poorly.

Real-World Examples

- Spotify: Spotify uses resource requests and limits to ensure its music streaming and recommendation services have the necessary resources to handle millions of users.
- Airbnb: Airbnb carefully manages resource allocation for its machine learning workloads, using requests and limits to optimize performance and control costs.
- Netflix: Netflix uses resource quotas to limit the amount of resources that different teams and applications can consume, ensuring fair allocation and preventing resource contention.

By understanding and effectively using resource requests and limits, you can ensure your machine learning applications run smoothly and efficiently on Kubernetes, even under heavy load.

6.2 Auto Scaling Machine Learning Applications

Let's talk about scaling! Think of your machine learning application like a popular restaurant. During peak hours, you need more chefs, waiters, and tables to handle the influx of customers. But during off-peak hours, you don't need as much staff or space.

Similarly, your machine learning application needs to scale up or down based on the demand for its predictions. You don't want to over-provision resources and pay for capacity you don't need, but you also don't want to under-provision and risk your application crashing or performing poorly under heavy load.

This is where autoscaling comes in. Kubernetes provides powerful autoscaling features that can automatically adjust the resources allocated to your application based on its actual usage. It's like having a smart manager who constantly monitors the restaurant and adjusts the staffing levels based on the number of customers.

Horizontal Pod Autoscaler (HPA)

The Horizontal Pod Autoscaler (HPA) is a Kubernetes resource that automatically scales the number of pods in a Deployment or ReplicaSet based on observed metrics. It's like adding more chefs to the kitchen when the orders start piling up.

How HPA Works

1. Metrics: The HPA monitors metrics like CPU utilization, memory usage, or custom metrics that you define.
2. Target: You set a target value for the metric (e.g., 50% CPU utilization).

3. Scaling: If the observed metric exceeds the target, the HPA increases the number of pods. If the metric falls below the target, the HPA decreases the number of pods.

Example:

YAML

```yaml
apiVersion: autoscaling/v2beta2
kind: HorizontalPodAutoscaler
metadata:
  name: my-ml-hpa
spec:
  scaleTargetRef:
    apiVersion: apps/v1
    kind: Deployment
    name: my-ml-deployment
  minReplicas: 2
  maxReplicas: 10
  metrics:
  - type: Resource
    resource:
      name: cpu
      target:
        type: Utilization
        averageUtilization:[1] 50
```

This HPA scales the my-ml-deployment Deployment between 2 and 10 replicas based on the average CPU utilization of the pods. If the average CPU utilization goes above 50%, the HPA will add more replicas. If it drops below 50%, it will remove some replicas.

Benefits of HPA

- Automatic scaling: You don't need to manually adjust the number of replicas as your application's traffic changes.
- Efficiency: HPA ensures that your application has the right amount of resources to handle the current workload, preventing over-provisioning and under-provisioning.
- Improved performance: HPA can improve your application's performance by ensuring it has enough resources to handle peak loads.

Vertical Pod Autoscaler (VPA)

The Vertical Pod Autoscaler (VPA) automatically adjusts the resource requests and limits of your pods based on their actual resource usage. It's like upgrading the kitchen equipment to handle more complex dishes or larger quantities of food.

How VPA Works

1. Monitoring: The VPA monitors the resource usage of your pods over time.
2. Recommendation: It analyzes the usage patterns and recommends new resource requests and limits.
3. Update: It updates the pod's resource requests and limits, either automatically or with your approval.

Benefits of VPA

- Optimized resource allocation: VPA ensures that your pods have the right amount of resources, preventing resource waste and contention.
- Simplified resource management: You don't need to manually tune resource requests and limits.
- Improved performance: VPA can improve your application's performance by ensuring it has the optimal amount of resources.

When to Use HPA vs. VPA

- HPA: Use HPA when you need to scale the *number* of replicas of your application based on metrics like CPU utilization or memory usage.
- VPA: Use VPA when you need to adjust the *amount* of resources allocated to each replica based on its actual usage.

Often, you can use both HPA and VPA together for comprehensive autoscaling.

Real-World Examples

- Spotify: Spotify uses HPA to automatically scale its music streaming and recommendation services based on user demand.
- Airbnb: Airbnb uses VPA to optimize the resource allocation for its machine learning workloads, reducing costs and improving efficiency.
- Pinterest: Pinterest uses a combination of HPA and VPA to scale its image recognition and recommendation services, ensuring high availability and performance.

By leveraging Kubernetes' autoscaling capabilities, you can build machine learning applications that dynamically adapt to changing workloads, ensuring optimal performance and cost efficiency.

6.3 Optimizing Resource Allocation for Cost Efficiency

Cloud computing can be incredibly powerful and convenient, but it can also get expensive if you're not careful. Think of it like running a household – you want to use electricity and water wisely to keep your utility bills down, right?

Similarly, in Kubernetes, you want to optimize your resource allocation to minimize costs while ensuring your machine learning applications perform well. It's about finding the sweet spot between performance and cost-effectiveness.

Why Optimize Resource Allocation?

- Reduce costs: Cloud providers charge for the resources you consume, so optimizing your resource usage can significantly reduce your cloud bill.
- Improve efficiency: Efficient resource allocation ensures that you're not wasting resources and that your applications have the resources they need when they need them.
- Environmental impact: Optimizing resource usage can also reduce your environmental footprint by minimizing energy consumption.

Techniques for Optimizing Resource Allocation

Here are some practical techniques for optimizing your resource allocation in Kubernetes:

1. Right-Size Your Requests and Limits

Don't over-request or over-limit resources. It's like ordering more food than you can eat – it's wasteful and costly. Analyze your application's resource usage patterns and set appropriate requests and limits.

- Monitoring: Use monitoring tools like Prometheus and Grafana to track your application's CPU and memory usage over time.
- Analysis: Analyze the monitoring data to understand your application's typical and peak resource consumption.
- Adjustment: Adjust your resource requests and limits based on your analysis.

2. Leverage the Vertical Pod Autoscaler (VPA)

The Vertical Pod Autoscaler (VPA) can be your automated resource manager. It analyzes your application's resource usage and automatically adjusts the resource requests and limits of your pods. This helps to optimize resource allocation without manual intervention.

3. Choose the Right Instance Types

Cloud providers offer a wide variety of instance types with different CPU, memory, and storage configurations. Choose the instance types that best match your application's needs.

- Consider your workload: If your application is CPU-intensive, choose an instance type with more CPU cores. If it's memory-intensive, choose an instance type with more memory.
- Optimize for cost: Compare the pricing of different instance types and choose the most cost-effective option for your needs.

4. Use Spot Instances (When Appropriate)

Spot instances are spare compute capacity in the cloud offered at a significantly lower price than on-demand instances. However, spot instances can be interrupted with short notice if the cloud provider needs the capacity back.

- Fault tolerance: Spot instances are a good option for fault-tolerant workloads that can handle interruptions.
- Cost savings: You can save a significant amount of money by using spot instances for non-critical workloads.

5. Optimize Your Application Code

Sometimes, the best way to optimize resource allocation is to optimize your application code itself.

- Efficient algorithms: Use efficient algorithms and data structures to reduce your application's resource consumption.

- Code profiling: Use code profiling tools to identify performance bottlenecks and optimize your code.
- Caching: Implement caching to reduce the number of computations and data accesses.

6. Monitor Your Resource Usage

Continuously monitor your resource usage to identify areas for optimization. Use monitoring tools and dashboards to track your spending, identify trends, and detect anomalies.

Real-World Examples

- Airbnb: Airbnb uses a combination of techniques, including right-sizing resource requests and limits, using the VPA, and optimizing its application code, to reduce its cloud costs while maintaining high performance.
- Pinterest: Pinterest uses spot instances for its batch processing and data analysis workloads, saving significant costs compared to on-demand instances.
- Lyft: Lyft uses a custom-built resource optimization platform to analyze its resource usage and make data-driven decisions about resource allocation.

By implementing these resource optimization techniques, you can effectively manage your cloud costs and ensure your machine learning applications are running efficiently and cost-effectively on Kubernetes.

6.4 GPU Management and Acceleration

In machine learning, training and running complex models can be computationally intensive. It's like trying to solve a massive jigsaw puzzle by hand – it can take a long time and a lot of effort.

But what if you had a special tool that could help you solve the puzzle much faster? That's where GPUs (Graphics Processing Units) come in. They're specialized hardware designed for parallel processing, making them ideal for accelerating machine learning workloads.

Think of a GPU as a team of workers who can tackle different parts of the puzzle simultaneously, speeding up the overall process. Similarly, GPUs can perform many calculations in parallel, drastically reducing the time it takes to train and run your models.

Kubernetes provides excellent support for managing and utilizing GPUs in your machine learning applications. Let's explore how it works:

1. Requesting and Limiting GPU Resources

Just like you can request and limit CPU and memory resources for your containers, you can also request and limit GPU resources. This ensures that your pods are scheduled on nodes with available GPUs and that they don't consume more GPU resources than they're allowed.

Example:

```yaml
apiVersion: v1
kind: Pod
metadata:
  name: my-ml-pod
spec:
  containers:
  - name: my-ml-container
    image: my-ml-image:latest
```

```
  resources:
    limits:
      nvidia.com/gpu: 1   # Request 1 GPU
```

In this example, the container requests one GPU using the nvidia.com/gpu resource name.

2. Scheduling Pods on Nodes with GPUs

You can use node selectors to ensure that your pods are scheduled on nodes with available GPUs. Node selectors are labels that you apply to nodes, and you can then specify in your pod definition that the pod should only be scheduled on nodes with those labels.

Example:

YAML

```
apiVersion: v1
kind: Pod
metadata:
  name: my-ml-pod
spec:
  containers:
  - name: my-ml-container
    image: my-ml-image:latest
  nodeSelector:
    accelerator: nvidia-tesla-k80   # Schedule on nodes with this label
```

3. Using Device Plugins

Kubernetes supports device plugins, which allow you to manage and allocate specialized hardware like GPUs. The NVIDIA device plugin is a popular choice for managing NVIDIA GPUs in Kubernetes.

The device plugin makes GPUs available as resources in Kubernetes, allowing you to request and limit them in your pod definitions.

4. Optimizing GPU Usage

To get the most out of your GPUs, you might need to optimize your machine learning code and framework.

- Batch size: Experiment with different batch sizes to find the optimal balance between GPU utilization and training speed.
- Data loading: Optimize your data loading pipeline to keep your GPUs fed with data.
- Framework optimization: Use framework-specific optimizations to maximize GPU performance.

Benefits of Using GPUs with Kubernetes

- Accelerated training: GPUs can significantly speed up model training, allowing you to iterate faster and experiment with more complex models.
- Improved performance: GPUs can also improve the performance of your deployed models, reducing latency and increasing throughput.
- Cost-effectiveness: While GPUs can be expensive, Kubernetes helps you utilize them efficiently, maximizing their value.

Real-World Examples

- Tesla: Tesla uses GPUs and Kubernetes to train and deploy its self-driving car models, leveraging the parallel processing power of GPUs to handle the massive amounts of data generated by its fleet of vehicles.
- Facebook: Facebook uses GPUs and Kubernetes to power its machine learning infrastructure, including its image recognition, natural language processing, and recommendation systems.
- OpenAI: OpenAI uses GPUs and Kubernetes to train its large language models, such as GPT-3, which require significant computational resources.

Effectively managing and utilizing GPUs with Kubernetes, you can unlock the full potential of your machine learning applications and achieve significant performance gains.

Chapter 7: Managing Machine Learning Pipelines

You've built your machine learning models, packaged them into containers, and deployed them on Kubernetes. But the journey doesn't end there! Machine learning models are dynamic entities that need to be continuously trained, evaluated, and updated to maintain their accuracy and effectiveness.

Think of it like tending a garden. You need to water the plants, provide nutrients, prune them regularly, and protect them from pests to keep them healthy and flourishing. Similarly, managing your machine learning pipelines involves a continuous cycle of experimentation, refinement, and deployment to ensure your models remain relevant and performant.

This chapter explores how to effectively manage your machine learning pipelines on Kubernetes, covering essential aspects like continuous integration and continuous delivery (CI/CD), experiment tracking, model versioning, and promoting models to production.

7.1 CI/CD for Machine Learning Workflows

CI/CD stands for Continuous Integration and Continuous Delivery (or Continuous Deployment). It's a set of practices that automate the process of building, testing, and deploying software. Think of it like an automated assembly line for your machine learning models. You feed in your code, data, and configurations, and the CI/CD pipeline takes care of the rest, from building and testing to deploying your model to production.

Why is CI/CD Important for Machine Learning?

- Speed and Agility: CI/CD automates many of the manual steps involved in building and deploying machine learning models, allowing you to iterate faster and get your models to production more quickly.
- Increased Collaboration: CI/CD enables multiple team members to work on the same project simultaneously without stepping on each other's toes. Changes are integrated continuously, reducing the risk of conflicts and integration headaches.
- Improved Reliability: Automated tests are a key part of CI/CD. This ensures that your code, data, and models are thoroughly tested before being deployed, reducing the risk of errors and bugs in production.
- Reduced Risk: By automating the deployment process, you minimize the risk of human error and ensure consistency across different environments.
- Faster Feedback Loops: CI/CD provides faster feedback loops, allowing you to identify and address issues early in the development cycle.

Key Components of a CI/CD Pipeline for Machine Learning

1. Version Control: The foundation of any CI/CD pipeline is a robust version control system like Git. You store your code, data, and model configurations in a Git repository, allowing you to track changes, collaborate with others, and revert to previous versions if needed.
2. Automated Build: A CI/CD tool like Jenkins, CircleCI, or GitLab CI/CD automatically builds your machine learning pipeline whenever changes are pushed to your Git repository. This typically involves:
    - Building a Docker image containing your updated model and application code.
    - Running any necessary data preprocessing for feature engineering steps.

- Training your machine learning model using the latest data.
3. **Automated Testing:** Automated tests are essential for ensuring the quality and reliability of your machine learning pipeline. These tests can include:
    - Unit tests: Test individual components of your code.
    - Integration tests: Test the interaction between different components.
    - Data tests: Validate the quality and integrity of your data.
    - Model tests: Evaluate the performance of your trained model using metrics like accuracy, precision, and recall.
4. **Automated Deployment:** Kubernetes plays a crucial role in automating the deployment of your machine learning models. You can use Kubernetes to:
    - Deploy your model to different environments, such as staging and production.
    - Implement different deployment strategies, such as rolling updates or canary deployments, to minimize disruption to your users.
    - Scale your deployments up or down based on demand.

Example CI/CD Workflow

Let's walk through a typical CI/CD workflow for a machine learning project:

1. **Code Change:** A data scientist updates the model training code or adds new features.
2. **Commit and Push:** The changes are committed to the Git repository and pushed to a central server.
3. **Trigger:** The CI/CD tool detects the code change and triggers a new build.

4. Build: The CI/CD tool builds a new Docker image containing the updated code and model.
5. Test: Automated tests are executed to validate the changes. If any tests fail, the pipeline stops, and the developer is notified.
6. Deploy to Staging: If all tests pass, the new image is deployed to a staging environment, which is a replica of the production environment used for testing and validation.
7. Manual Approval (Optional): You might have a manual approval step before deploying to production. This allows you to review the changes and ensure they meet your quality standards.
8. Deploy to Production: Once approved, the new image is automatically deployed to the production environment, making the updated model available to users.

Tools for CI/CD

- Jenkins: A popular open-source automation server that can be used to build and manage CI/CD pipelines.
- CircleCI: A cloud-based CI/CD platform that offers a user-friendly interface and integrates with various tools and services.
- GitLab CI/CD: A built-in CI/CD system within GitLab that provides a seamless workflow for building, testing, and deploying code.
- Argo CD: A declarative, GitOps continuous delivery tool for Kubernetes.

Real-World Examples

- Netflix: Netflix uses a sophisticated CI/CD pipeline to automate the training, evaluation, and deployment of its recommendation models, allowing it to quickly iterate and improve its algorithms.

- Uber: Uber uses CI/CD to ensure the reliability and scalability of its machine learning models for fraud detection, ETA prediction, and other critical services.
- Spotify: Spotify uses CI/CD to streamline the development and deployment of its machine learning models for music recommendation and personalization.

By adopting CI/CD practices for your machine learning workflows, you can accelerate your development cycle, improve collaboration, and increase the reliability of your deployments.

7.2 Experiment Tracking and Artifact Management

Machine learning is an iterative process. You constantly experiment with different algorithms, hyperparameters, data preprocessing techniques, and feature engineering strategies to find the best approach for your problem. It's like being a chef trying different ingredients and cooking methods to create the perfect dish.

But how do you keep track of all these experiments? How do you remember which ingredients and methods you used for each attempt? How do you compare the results and determine which approach worked best?

This is where experiment tracking and artifact management come in. They provide a systematic way to record your experiments, track their parameters and results, and manage the artifacts generated during the process.

Think of it like keeping a detailed lab notebook where you meticulously record every experiment, every ingredient used, every measurement taken, and every observation made. This allows you to reproduce your experiments, analyze your results, and draw meaningful conclusions.

Why is Experiment Tracking Important?

- Reproducibility: In machine learning, it's crucial to be able to reproduce your experiments. This allows you to verify your results, debug issues, and collaborate with others. Experiment tracking helps you capture all the necessary information to recreate an experiment precisely.
- Comparison and Analysis: By tracking your experiments, you can easily compare the results of different approaches and analyze the impact of different parameters on your model's performance. This helps you make data-driven decisions and choose the best approach for your problem.
- Collaboration: Experiment tracking facilitates collaboration by providing a shared record of experiments and their results. This allows team members to understand each other's work, share insights, and build upon previous experiments.
- Knowledge Sharing: A well-maintained experiment tracking system can serve as a valuable knowledge base for your team, capturing the history of your experiments and the lessons learned along the way.

Key Components of Experiment Tracking

- Experiment parameters: Record the hyperparameters, data versions, code versions, and other settings used in each experiment.
- Metrics: Track the performance of each experiment using relevant metrics, such as accuracy, precision, recall, F1-score, AUC, and loss.
- Artifacts: Store the trained models, evaluation results, visualizations, and other artifacts generated by each experiment.
- Code versioning: Integrate with your version control system (e.g., Git) to track the code used in each experiment.
- Notes and tags: Add notes and tags to your experiments to provide context and organize your work.

Tools for Experiment Tracking and Artifact Management

Several tools can help you with experiment tracking and artifact management:

- MLflow: An open-source platform for managing the entire machine learning lifecycle, including experiment tracking, artifact management, model registry, and deployment.
- Weights & Biases: A cloud-based platform that provides a user-friendly interface for tracking experiments, visualizing results, and collaborating with others.
- TensorBoard: A visualization tool for TensorFlow that can also be used for experiment tracking and visualizing metrics.
- Comet: A cloud-based platform for tracking experiments, visualizing results, and comparing different models.

Example using MLflow:

```python
Python

import mlflow

# Start an MLflow run

with mlflow.start_run():

    # Log parameters

    mlflow.log_param("learning_rate", 0.01)

    mlflow.log_param("batch_size", 32)

    # ... train your model ...

    # Log metrics

    mlflow.log_metric("accuracy", 0.95)
```

```
mlflow.log_metric("f1_score", 0.92)

# Log artifacts

mlflow.log_artifact("model.pkl")

mlflow.log_artifact("confusion_matrix.png")
```

This code snippet demonstrates how to use MLflow to track an experiment. It logs the learning rate and batch size as parameters, the accuracy and F1-score as metrics, and the trained model (model.pkl) and a confusion matrix plot (confusion_matrix.png) as artifacts.

Integrating with Kubernetes

You can integrate your experiment tracking tools with Kubernetes to streamline your workflow. For example, you can:

- Run MLflow on Kubernetes: Deploy MLflow as a service on your Kubernetes cluster.
- Log experiment metadata to Kubernetes: Use Kubernetes annotations or custom resources to store experiment metadata alongside your deployments.
- Trigger experiments from Kubernetes: Use Kubernetes Jobs or CronJobs to trigger experiments and track their progress.

Real-World Examples

- Netflix: Netflix uses MLflow to track experiments, manage artifacts, and deploy models for its recommendation systems.
- Uber: Uber uses a combination of internal tools and open-source platforms like TensorBoard to track experiments and visualize results.
- Airbnb: Airbnb uses a custom-built experiment tracking system that integrates with its Kubernetes infrastructure.

By implementing robust experiment tracking and artifact management practices, you can gain valuable insights from your experiments, improve collaboration, and accelerate your machine learning development cycle.

7.3 Model Registry and Version Control

You've trained a bunch of machine learning models, experimented with different approaches, and carefully tracked your progress. Now, you need a place to store these models, manage their versions, and make them easily accessible for deployment and collaboration. This is where a model registry comes in.

Think of a model registry like a well-organized library for your machine learning models. It's a central repository where you can store, version, and manage your models, ensuring they're readily available when you need them.

Why is a Model Registry Important?

- Organization and Discoverability: As you train more and more models, it becomes crucial to organize them effectively. A model registry provides a central place to store your models and their associated metadata, making it easy to find and retrieve the models you need.
- Version Control: Machine learning models evolve over time. You might retrain your models with new data, fine-tune their hyperparameters, or experiment with different architectures. A model registry allows you to version your models, keeping track of different iterations and their performance metrics.
- Deployment: A model registry can streamline your deployment process by providing a single source of truth for your models. You can easily deploy specific versions of your models to different environments, such as staging or production.

- Collaboration: A model registry facilitates collaboration by allowing team members to share models, access previous versions, and understand the evolution of a model over time.
- Reproducibility: By storing your models and their associated metadata, a model registry helps ensure the reproducibility of your experiments and deployments.

Key Features of a Model Registry

- Model storage: A place to store your trained models, typically in a format that can be easily loaded and used for inference.
- Versioning: Ability to track different versions of your models and their associated metadata, such as training data, hyperparameters, and performance metrics.
- Metadata management: Ability to store and query metadata about your models, such as training date, author, and evaluation results.
- Access control: Control who can access and modify your models.
- Deployment integration: Integration with deployment tools and platforms, such as Kubernetes, to streamline the deployment process.

Tools for Model Registry and Version Control

Several tools can help you implement a model registry:

- MLflow Model Registry: An open-source component of MLflow that provides a centralized model store with versioning, staging, and deployment capabilities.
- TensorFlow Hub: A repository of pre-trained TensorFlow models that can also be used to store and share your own models.

- AWS SageMaker Model Registry: A fully managed service from AWS for storing, versioning, and deploying machine learning models.
- Azure Machine Learning Model Registry: A similar service from Azure that provides a central repository for managing your models.

Example using MLflow Model Registry:

Python

```python
import mlflow
# ... train your model ...
# Log the model to MLflow
model_uri = "runs:/{}/my-model".format(mlflow.active_run().info.run_id)
# Register the model in the Model Registry
mv = mlflow.register_model(model_uri, "MyModel")
# Transition the model to "Production" stage
client = mlflow.tracking.MlflowClient()
client.transition_model_version_stage(
    name="MyModel",
    version=mv.version,
    stage="Production",
)
```

This code snippet shows how to use MLflow to register a model in the Model Registry and transition it to the "Production" stage.

Integrating with Kubernetes

You can integrate your model registry with Kubernetes to streamline your deployment workflow. For example, you can:

- Deploy your model registry on Kubernetes: Run your model registry as a service on your Kubernetes cluster.
- Access models from Kubernetes: Configure your Kubernetes deployments to fetch models from your model registry.
- Automate deployments: Use Kubernetes to automate the deployment of new model versions from your registry.

Real-World Examples

- Netflix: Netflix uses a custom-built model registry to manage and deploy its vast collection of machine learning models for personalized recommendations.
- Uber: Uber leverages a model registry to track different versions of its machine learning models for fraud detection, ETA prediction, and other services.
- Airbnb: Airbnb uses a model registry to manage and deploy its models for search ranking, pricing optimization, and other applications.

Implementing a robust model registry and version control system, you can effectively manage your machine learning models, streamline your deployment process, and ensure reproducibility and collaboration in your projects.

7.4 Promoting Models to Production

You've trained a champion model, meticulously tracked its performance, and carefully stored it in your model registry. Now, it's time for the grand finale: promoting your model to production! This is where your model graduates from the training grounds and enters the real world, where it will interact with live data and generate predictions for users or other applications.

Think of it like an athlete preparing for a major competition. They train rigorously, hone their skills, and compete in smaller events to prepare for the big stage. Similarly, your model goes through various stages of development and testing before it's ready to perform in the production environment.

Promoting a model to production is a critical step that requires careful planning and execution. It's about ensuring a smooth transition, minimizing disruption to your users, and maintaining the quality and reliability of your application.

Key Considerations for Promoting Models to Production

- Model Validation: Before deploying your model to production, you need to thoroughly validate its performance. This involves evaluating its accuracy, precision, recall, and other relevant metrics on a held-out dataset that it hasn't seen before. This helps ensure that your model generalizes well to new data and performs as expected in the real world.
- Staging Environment: A staging environment is a replica of your production environment where you can test your model before deploying it to live users. This allows you to catch any integration issues or performance bottlenecks before they impact your users.
- Testing: Thorough testing is essential before promoting your model to production. This includes unit tests, integration tests, and end-to-end tests to ensure your model works correctly and integrates seamlessly with other systems.
- Monitoring: Once your model is in production, you need to continuously monitor its performance and health. This helps you detect any issues, such as model drift or performance degradation, and take corrective action before they impact your users.

- Rollbacks: Have a plan in place to roll back to a previous version of your model if necessary. This allows you to quickly revert to a known good state if you encounter any issues with the new version.

Deployment Strategies for Promoting Models

Several deployment strategies can help you safely and effectively promote your models to production:

- Blue/Green Deployments: This strategy involves deploying the new version of your model (green) alongside the old version (blue). You then gradually switch traffic from the blue deployment to the green deployment. Once you're confident in the new version's performance, you can decommission the blue deployment.
- Canary Deployments: This strategy involves gradually rolling out the new version of your model to a small subset of users or traffic. You monitor the performance of the new version and gradually increase the traffic to it if it performs well. This allows you to catch any issues or regressions before they impact a large number of users.
- A/B Testing: This strategy involves deploying multiple versions of your model and routing a portion of your traffic to each version. You then monitor the performance of each version and compare their metrics to determine which one performs better. This allows you to experiment with different approaches and gather data on their effectiveness before committing to a particular version.

Kubernetes for Promoting Models to Production

Kubernetes provides excellent support for implementing these deployment strategies. You can use Kubernetes Deployments to manage the rollout and updates of your models, Services to route traffic to different versions, and Ingress to manage external access.

Example: Blue/Green Deployment with Kubernetes

1. Deploy the new version: Create a new Deployment for the new version of your model.
2. Create a new Service: Create a new Service that targets the new Deployment.
3. Update the Ingress: Update your Ingress resource to route traffic to the new Service.
4. Monitor: Monitor the performance of the new version.
5. Decommission the old version: Once you're confident in the new version, delete the old Deployment and Service.

Real-World Examples

- Netflix: Netflix uses canary deployments and A/B testing to safely roll out new versions of its recommendation models to its massive user base.
- Uber: Uber uses blue/green deployments to ensure high availability and minimize downtime when updating its machine learning models for fraud detection and ETA prediction.
- Airbnb: Airbnb uses a combination of deployment strategies, including canary deployments and A/B testing, to promote new versions of its search ranking and pricing models.

By carefully planning your promotion strategy and leveraging the capabilities of Kubernetes, you can ensure a smooth and successful transition for your machine learning models from development to production.

Chapter 8: Security and Access Control

We've covered a lot of ground in building, deploying, and managing machine learning applications on Kubernetes. But there's one crucial aspect we can't overlook: security! Think of it like protecting your valuable possessions. You wouldn't leave your house unlocked or your valuables out in the open, right? You'd take measures to secure your belongings and prevent unauthorized access.

Similarly, securing your Kubernetes cluster and machine learning applications is essential for protecting your valuable data, models, and intellectual property. This chapter explores the key security considerations and best practices for building and deploying secure machine learning applications on Kubernetes.

8.1 Securing Your Kubernetes Cluster

Your Kubernetes cluster is the heart of your machine learning operations. It's where your valuable data, models, and applications reside. Think of it like a fortress that needs strong defenses to protect its precious contents from intruders.

Securing your Kubernetes cluster is not just about preventing malicious attacks. It's also about ensuring the reliability, integrity, and availability of your applications and data. It's about building a solid foundation of trust and confidence in your machine learning infrastructure.

Why is Kubernetes Cluster Security Important?

- Protect sensitive data: Your cluster might handle sensitive data, such as personal information, financial records, or

medical data. A security breach could expose this data to unauthorized access, leading to privacy violations, legal liabilities, and reputational damage.
- Prevent unauthorized access: Attackers could gain control of your cluster and use it for malicious purposes, such as launching attacks on other systems, stealing data, or disrupting your operations.
- Ensure application integrity: Attackers could tamper with your applications or inject malicious code, compromising their functionality and potentially harming your users.
- Maintain availability: A security incident could disrupt your cluster's operations, leading to downtime and impacting your business.

Key Areas to Secure

Securing your Kubernetes cluster involves a multi-faceted approach. Let's break down the key areas you need to focus on:

1. Control Plane Security

The control plane is the brain of your Kubernetes cluster. It manages all the cluster's operations, including scheduling pods, managing resources, and enforcing policies. Protecting the control plane is paramount.

- Restrict API Server Access: The API server is the central point of communication for all Kubernetes components and users. Limit access to the API server to authorized users and applications only. Use strong authentication and authorization mechanisms like role-based access control (RBAC).
- Enable Encryption: Encrypt all communication between the control plane components and between the control plane and worker nodes using Transport Layer Security (TLS). This prevents eavesdropping and tampering with sensitive data.

- Regular Updates: Keep your Kubernetes version up-to-date with the latest security patches. New vulnerabilities are constantly being discovered, and staying up-to-date is crucial for mitigating these risks.

2. Worker Node Security

Worker nodes are the workhorses of your cluster, where your applications run. Securing them is essential for protecting your workloads.

- Hardening the Operating System: Use a minimal operating system image for your worker nodes and keep it updated with the latest security patches. This reduces the attack surface and minimizes the risk of vulnerabilities.
- Network Security: Configure firewalls to restrict network access to your worker nodes. Only allow necessary traffic and block all other incoming and outgoing connections.
- Security Auditing: Regularly audit your worker nodes for security vulnerabilities and misconfigurations. Use security scanning tools to identify potential weaknesses and address them promptly.

3. Network Policies

Network policies allow you to control network traffic between pods in your cluster. This helps to isolate your applications and prevent unauthorized access.

- Define Policies: Create network policies that specify which pods can communicate with each other. You can define policies based on labels, namespaces, or IP addresses.
- Deny by Default: Use a "deny by default" policy to block all traffic that is not explicitly allowed. This helps to minimize the impact of a security breach by limiting the lateral movement of attackers.

Example Network Policy:

```yaml
apiVersion: networking.k8s.io/v1
kind: NetworkPolicy
metadata:
  name: deny-all
spec:
  podSelector: {}  # Select all pods
  policyTypes:
  - Ingress
  - Egress
```

This policy denies all incoming and outgoing traffic to all pods in the namespace.

4. Secrets Management

Kubernetes secrets provide a secure way to store sensitive information, such as API keys, passwords, and certificates.

- Use Secrets: Always store your sensitive data in Kubernetes secrets instead of hardcoding them in your application code or configuration files.
- Limit Access: Control access to secrets using RBAC. Only grant access to users and applications that require it.

Example Secret:

```yaml
apiVersion: v1
kind: Secret
```

```
metadata:
  name: my-secret
type: Opaque
data:
  api-key: <base64-encoded API key>
```

Real-World Examples

- Financial Institutions: Banks and other financial institutions use Kubernetes to run their critical applications, implementing strict security measures to protect sensitive financial data and comply with regulations like PCI DSS.
- Healthcare Organizations: Healthcare providers use Kubernetes to manage patient data and deploy machine learning models for diagnosis and treatment, adhering to HIPAA regulations for data privacy and security.
- Government Agencies: Government agencies use Kubernetes to secure sensitive information and deploy applications for national security and intelligence, implementing strict access controls and security audits.

By implementing these security measures and best practices, you can build a robust and secure Kubernetes cluster, providing a solid foundation for your machine learning applications and protecting your valuable data and resources.

8.2 Authentication and Authorization for ML Applications

In Kubernetes and machine learning, authentication and authorization are crucial for protecting your models, data, and infrastructure from unauthorized access and malicious activities.

Why are Authentication and Authorization Important for ML Applications?

- Protect sensitive data: Your ML applications might handle sensitive data, such as personal information, financial records, or medical data. Authentication and authorization help ensure that only authorized users and applications can access this data.
- Prevent unauthorized model access: Your trained machine learning models are valuable assets. Authentication and authorization help prevent unauthorized users from accessing, modifying, or deleting your models.
- Control access to resources: Your ML applications might consume significant resources, such as CPU, memory, and GPUs. Authentication and authorization help you control which users and applications can access these resources and prevent resource abuse.
- Enforce security policies: You can use authentication and authorization to enforce your organization's security policies and comply with regulations.

Authentication

Authentication is the process of verifying the identity of a user or application trying to access your system. It's like showing your ID card at the entrance to a secure building.

Kubernetes supports various authentication methods:

- Service Account Tokens: Service accounts are special Kubernetes accounts used by applications running within the cluster. Each service account is associated with a token that can be used for authentication.
- Static Token File: You can create a file containing a list of usernames and passwords (or tokens) and configure Kubernetes to use this file for authentication.

- Bootstrap Tokens: Bootstrap tokens are temporary tokens used to authenticate new nodes joining the cluster.
- X.509 Client Certificates: You can use X.509 client certificates to authenticate users and applications.
- OpenID Connect (OIDC): OIDC is an authentication protocol that allows you to integrate with identity providers like Google, Azure, or Okta.

Authorization

Authorization is the process of controlling what actions an authenticated user or application is allowed to perform. It's like having different levels of access within a building – some people might have access to all areas, while others might only be allowed in certain rooms.

Kubernetes provides several authorization mechanisms:

- Role-Based Access Control (RBAC): RBAC is the most commonly used authorization mechanism in Kubernetes. It allows you to define roles, which are sets of permissions, and assign those roles to users and applications.
- Attribute-Based Access Control (ABAC): ABAC is a more fine-grained authorization mechanism that allows you to define policies based on attributes of the user, the resource, and the environment.
- Webhooks: Webhooks allow you to delegate authorization decisions to an external service.

Example RBAC Configuration

Let's say you want to create a role that allows a user to read and list machine learning models in a specific namespace. Here's how you can do it using RBAC:

```yaml
apiVersion: rbac.authorization.k8s.io/v1
```

```yaml
kind: Role
metadata:
  namespace: my-ml-namespace
  name: ml-model-reader
rules:
- apiGroups: ["machinelearning.io"] # Replace with your API group
  resources: ["models"]
  verbs: ["get", "list"]
---
apiVersion: rbac.authorization.k8s.io/v1
kind: RoleBinding
metadata:
  name: read-models
  namespace: my-ml-namespace
subjects:
- kind: User
  name: bob  # Replace with the actual username
  apiGroup: rbac.authorization.k8s.io
roleRef:
  kind: Role
```

```
name: ml-model-reader

apiGroup: rbac.authorization.k8s.io
```

This configuration creates a role named ml-model-reader that allows reading and listing models in the my-ml-namespace namespace. It then creates a role binding that grants this role to the user "bob."

Best Practices for Authentication and Authorization

- Principle of Least Privilege: Grant users and applications only the minimum necessary permissions to perform their tasks.
- Use Strong Authentication: Use strong authentication methods, such as multi-factor authentication, to protect against unauthorized access.[1]
- Regularly Review Permissions: Periodically review the permissions granted to users and applications to ensure they are still appropriate.
- Use Namespaces: Use namespaces to isolate different applications and users, limiting the impact of a security breach.

Real-World Examples

- Healthcare: Healthcare organizations use authentication and authorization to control access to sensitive patient data and ensure compliance with HIPAA regulations.
- Finance: Financial institutions use strong authentication and authorization mechanisms to protect financial data and prevent fraud.
- Government: Government agencies use RBAC and other authorization mechanisms to enforce strict access controls and protect classified information.

8.3 Protecting Sensitive Data in Machine Learning

Machine learning applications often deal with sensitive data, such as personal information, financial records, or medical histories. Protecting this data is not just a good practice; it's often a legal and ethical requirement.

Think of it like handling confidential documents. You wouldn't leave them lying around in the open or share them with unauthorized people, right? You'd take precautions to protect their confidentiality and prevent unauthorized access.

Similarly, protecting sensitive data in machine learning involves implementing measures to ensure data privacy, security, and compliance with relevant regulations.

Why is Protecting Sensitive Data Crucial?

- Privacy violations: A data breach could expose sensitive information, leading to privacy violations and potential harm to individuals.
- Legal and regulatory compliance: Many industries have strict regulations regarding the handling of sensitive data, such as the General Data Protection Regulation (GDPR) or the Health Insurance Portability and Accountability Act (HIPAA).[1] Failure to comply with these regulations can result in[2] hefty fines and legal penalties.
- Reputational damage: A data breach can damage your organization's reputation and erode trust with your customers.
- Ethical considerations: Protecting sensitive data is an ethical responsibility. As machine learning practitioners, we have a duty to handle data responsibly and safeguard the privacy of individuals.

Key Techniques for Protecting Sensitive Data

1. **Data Encryption:**

Encryption is a fundamental technique for protecting data. It involves converting data into a scrambled format that can only be deciphered with the correct decryption key.

- Encryption at rest: Encrypt your data when it's stored on disk or in a database. Kubernetes secrets can be used to store sensitive data securely, and you can also encrypt your persistent volumes.
- Encryption in transit: Encrypt your data when it's transmitted over the network. Use Transport Layer Security (TLS) to secure communication between your applications and services.

2. Access Control:

Restrict access to your data to authorized users and applications only.

- Role-Based Access Control (RBAC): Use RBAC to define roles and assign them to users and applications, granting them specific permissions to access and modify data.
- Network Policies: Use network policies to control network traffic between pods in your cluster, limiting access to your data stores to authorized applications.

3. Data Masking and Anonymization:

Data masking and anonymization techniques can help protect sensitive data while still allowing it to be used for machine learning.

- Masking: Replace sensitive data with realistic but fake data. For example, you could replace real names with pseudonyms or mask credit card numbers while preserving their format.
- Anonymization: Remove or generalize identifying information from your data. For example, you could remove

names and addresses or aggregate data to remove individual identifiers.

4. Data Provenance:

Data provenance involves tracking the origin and history of your data. This helps ensure the integrity and authenticity of your data and can be useful for auditing and compliance purposes.

- Data lineage: Track the transformations and processing steps applied to your data.
- Data versioning: Keep track of different versions of your data and their associated metadata.

5. Compliance with Regulations:

Ensure your machine learning applications comply with relevant data privacy regulations, such as GDPR, HIPAA, or CCPA.

- Data subject rights: Implement mechanisms to support data subject rights, such as the right to access, rectify, or erase their data.
- Data breach notification: Have a plan in place to notify affected individuals and authorities in case of a data breach.

Real-World Examples

- Healthcare: Healthcare organizations use encryption, access control, and de-identification techniques to protect sensitive patient data while using it for machine learning applications like disease prediction and personalized treatment.
- Finance: Financial institutions use encryption, access control, and fraud detection models to protect financial data and prevent unauthorized transactions.
- Self-driving cars: Autonomous vehicle companies use anonymization techniques to protect the privacy of individuals captured in their training data while still using the data to train their self-driving algorithms.

Best Practices for Protecting Sensitive Data

- Minimize data collection: Collect only the data that is necessary for your machine learning task.
- Data retention: Don't keep sensitive data longer than necessary.
- Data security training: Train your team on data security best practices and the importance of protecting sensitive information.
- Stay informed: Stay up-to-date on the latest data privacy regulations and best practices.

8.4 Security Best Practices for Kubernetes and ML

We've explored various security measures for your Kubernetes cluster and machine learning applications. Now, let's distill these into a set of actionable best practices that you can follow to build a robust and secure environment for your ML workloads.

Think of these best practices as your security checklist – a guide to ensure you've covered all the essential bases and minimized the risk of vulnerabilities and attacks.

1. Principle of Least Privilege

This fundamental security principle states that you should grant users and applications only the minimum necessary permissions to perform their tasks. Avoid granting excessive permissions, as this can increase the potential damage if an account is compromised.

- RBAC: Use Role-Based Access Control (RBAC) to define fine-grained roles and assign them to users and service accounts.
- Limit access to secrets: Grant access to Kubernetes secrets only to the applications that require them.

- Network policies: Use network policies to restrict communication between pods, limiting the blast radius of a potential attack.

2. Defense in Depth

Don't rely on a single security measure. Implement multiple layers of security to create a robust defense. It's like having multiple locks on your door – it makes it much harder for an intruder to break in.

- Network security: Configure firewalls and network policies to restrict access to your cluster and applications.
- Authentication and authorization: Use strong authentication and authorization mechanisms to verify the identity of users and applications and control their access to resources.
- Image scanning: Scan your container images for vulnerabilities before deploying them.
- Security auditing: Regularly audit your cluster and applications for security weaknesses and misconfigurations.

3. Regular Security Audits

Security is an ongoing process, not a one-time event. Regularly audit your Kubernetes cluster and machine learning applications for security vulnerabilities and misconfigurations.

- Vulnerability scanning: Use tools like Snyk or Clair to scan your container images for known vulnerabilities.
- Configuration auditing: Review your Kubernetes configurations, such as deployments, services, and ingress, to ensure they adhere to security best practices.
- Penetration testing: Conduct penetration tests to simulate real-world attacks and identify vulnerabilities in your system.

4. Security Training

Your team is your first line of defense. Train your team on security best practices for Kubernetes and machine learning.

- Kubernetes security training: Educate your team on Kubernetes security concepts, such as RBAC, network policies, and secrets management.
- Machine learning security training: Train your team on secure coding practices for machine learning, data privacy, and model security.
- Security awareness: Promote a culture of security awareness within your team, encouraging them to report potential security issues and stay informed about the latest threats.

5. Stay Up-to-Date

The world of technology is constantly evolving, and new security threats emerge regularly. Stay up-to-date with the latest security best practices and vulnerabilities.

- Kubernetes updates: Keep your Kubernetes version up-to-date with the latest security patches.
- Container image updates: Regularly update your container images to include the latest security fixes.
- Dependency updates: Keep your application dependencies up-to-date to patch known vulnerabilities.
- Security advisories: Subscribe to security advisories and mailing lists to stay informed about new threats and vulnerabilities.

Real-World Examples

- Google: Google uses a defense-in-depth approach to secure its Kubernetes infrastructure, implementing multiple layers of security, including network policies, authentication, authorization, and encryption.
- Microsoft: Microsoft uses a combination of automated and manual security audits to ensure the security of its Azure Kubernetes Service (AKS).

- Amazon: Amazon provides security training and resources to help its customers secure their Amazon Elastic Kubernetes Service (EKS) clusters.

By following these security best practices, you can build a secure and resilient environment for your machine learning applications on Kubernetes, protecting your valuable data and ensuring the integrity and availability of your services.

Chapter 9: Advanced Topics and Future Trends

We've covered a lot of ground in this book, from the basics of Kubernetes to deploying and scaling machine learning applications. But the world of cloud-native machine learning is constantly evolving, with new technologies and trends emerging all the time.

This chapter explores some of the advanced topics and future trends in this exciting field. Think of it as a glimpse into the future of machine learning, where we'll explore cutting-edge technologies and discuss how they might shape the way we build and deploy intelligent applications.

9.1 Serverless Machine Learning with Knative

In cloud computing, we're always looking for ways to optimize resource utilization and reduce costs. This is where serverless computing comes in. It's a cloud execution model where the cloud provider dynamically manages the allocation of machine resources. You, as the developer, focus solely on your code, and the cloud provider handles all the underlying infrastructure, scaling your application up or down as needed.

Think of it like ordering a ride from a ride-sharing service. You don't need to own a car or worry about maintenance, parking, or insurance. You simply request a ride, and the service takes care of the rest, providing a car and a driver to get you to your destination.

Similarly, with serverless computing, you don't need to manage servers, operating systems, or scaling infrastructure. You just deploy your code, and the cloud provider handles the rest, scaling your application automatically based on demand.

Knative is a Kubernetes-based platform that brings serverless capabilities to your machine learning workloads. It allows you to deploy your models as serverless functions that scale automatically based on demand. This means you only pay for the resources you actually use, and you don't have to worry about managing servers or infrastructure.

Why Serverless Machine Learning?

- Cost-efficiency: Pay only for the resources your model consumes when it's actively processing requests. No more paying for idle servers or over-provisioned capacity.
- Scalability: Your model can automatically scale up or down based on the incoming traffic. This ensures that your application can handle peak loads without performance degradation or downtime.
- Reduced operational overhead: You don't need to manage servers, operating systems, or scaling infrastructure. This frees up your time and resources to focus on developing and improving your models.
- Faster development: Serverless platforms like Knative simplify the deployment process, allowing you to get your models to production faster.

How Knative Works

Knative provides two main components for building serverless applications:

- Serving: Allows you to deploy your applications as scalable services. It handles the routing of requests to your application, scaling the number of instances based on demand, and managing the lifecycle of your deployments.

- Eventing: Enables event-driven architectures. It allows you to define event sources, triggers, and brokers, enabling your applications to respond to events from various sources, such as message queues or cloud storage services.

Deploying a Machine Learning Model with Knative

Let's say you have a trained TensorFlow model that you want to deploy as a serverless endpoint. Here's how you can do it using Knative Serving:

1. Package your model: Package your model and any necessary dependencies into a Docker image.
2. Create a Knative Service: Define a Knative Service YAML file that specifies your Docker image and any configuration parameters.

Example Knative Service YAML:

YAML

```yaml
apiVersion: serving.knative.dev/v1

kind: Service

metadata:
  name: my-tensorflow-model

spec:
  template:
    spec:
      containers:
        - image: my-tensorflow-model-image:latest
          ports:
```

```
      - containerPort: 8501  # The port your
model listens on
```

3. **Deploy the service:** Use the kubectl command to deploy your Knative Service to your Kubernetes cluster.

Bash

```
kubectl apply -f service.yaml
```

Knative will automatically create the necessary deployments, services, and routes to expose your model as a serverless endpoint.

Key Concepts in Knative

- Revision: A specific version of your application deployed by Knative.
- Configuration: Defines the desired state of your application, including the Docker image and any configuration parameters.
- Route: Maps a network endpoint to a specific Revision.

Benefits of Using Knative for Machine Learning

- Automatic scaling: Knative automatically scales your model deployments based on demand, ensuring optimal resource utilization and performance.
- Simplified deployment: Knative simplifies the deployment process, allowing you to focus on your model code rather than infrastructure management.
- Integration with Kubernetes: Knative builds on top of Kubernetes, leveraging its powerful orchestration capabilities and ecosystem of tools.

Real-World Examples

- OpenFaaS: OpenFaaS is a popular open-source serverless platform that uses Knative to provide serverless functions for machine learning and other workloads.

- Cloud Run: Google Cloud Run is a fully managed serverless platform that uses Knative to deploy and scale containerized applications, including machine learning models.
- TriggerMesh: TriggerMesh is a serverless management platform that uses Knative to connect applications and services through event-driven architectures.

Leveraging Knative and serverless technologies, you can build and deploy machine learning applications that are highly scalable, cost-effective, and efficient, allowing you to focus on what matters most: developing innovative and impactful models.

9.2 Using GPUs and Hardware Accelerators

Let's talk about speed! In machine learning, training and running complex models can be computationally demanding. It's like trying to analyze a massive dataset with a magnifying glass – it can take a long time and a lot of effort.

But what if you had a powerful microscope that could analyze the data much faster? That's where GPUs (Graphics Processing Units) and other hardware accelerators come in. They're specialized hardware designed for parallel processing, making them ideal for accelerating machine learning workloads.

Think of a GPU as a team of experts who can analyze different parts of the dataset simultaneously, speeding up the overall process. Similarly, GPUs can perform many calculations in parallel, drastically reducing the time it takes to train and run your models.

Why Use GPUs and Hardware Accelerators?

- Faster Training: GPUs can significantly accelerate the training of machine learning models, especially for deep learning models with millions or even billions of

parameters. This allows you to iterate faster, experiment with more complex models, and achieve better results.
- **Improved Performance:** GPUs can also enhance the performance of your deployed models, reducing latency and increasing throughput. This is crucial for real-time applications that require quick responses, such as image recognition or natural language processing.
- **Cost-Effectiveness:** While GPUs and other hardware accelerators can be expensive, they can also be more cost-effective in the long run by reducing the time and resources required for training and inference.

How Kubernetes Manages GPUs and Accelerators

Kubernetes provides excellent support for managing and utilizing GPUs and other hardware accelerators in your machine learning applications.

- **Resource Requests and Limits:** You can request and limit GPU resources for your containers, just like you do for CPU and memory. This ensures that your pods are scheduled on nodes with available GPUs and that they don't consume more GPU resources than they're allowed.

Example:

YAML

```
apiVersion: v1
kind: Pod
metadata:
  name: my-ml-pod
spec:
  containers:
  - name: my-ml-container
```

```
      image: my-ml-image:latest
    resources:
      limits:
        nvidia.com/gpu: 1   # Request 1 GPU
```

- **Node Selectors:** You can use node selectors to ensure that your pods are scheduled on nodes with specific hardware capabilities. This allows you to target pods that require GPUs to nodes that have GPUs installed.

Example:

YAML

```
apiVersion: v1
kind: Pod
metadata:
  name: my-ml-pod
spec:
  containers:
  - name: my-ml-container
    image: my-ml-image:latest
  nodeSelector:
    accelerator: nvidia-tesla-k80   # Schedule on nodes with this label
```

- **Device Plugins:** Kubernetes supports device plugins, which allow you to manage and allocate specialized hardware resources like GPUs. The NVIDIA device plugin is a popular choice for managing NVIDIA GPUs in Kubernetes. It allows Kubernetes to discover and allocate GPUs to your pods.

Optimizing GPU Usage

To get the most out of your GPUs, you might need to optimize your machine learning code and framework.

- Batch Size: Experiment with different batch sizes to find the optimal balance between GPU utilization and training speed. Larger batch sizes can improve GPU utilization, but they might also increase memory usage and training time.
- Data Loading: Optimize your data loading pipeline to keep your GPUs fed with data. Use techniques like prefetching and caching to minimize data loading time and avoid GPU starvation.
- Framework Optimization: Use framework-specific optimizations to maximize GPU performance. For example, TensorFlow provides the XLA (Accelerated Linear Algebra) compiler, which can optimize your TensorFlow graphs for specific hardware.

Types of Hardware Accelerators

- GPUs: General-purpose graphics processing units are widely used for machine learning due to their parallel processing capabilities.
- TPUs: Tensor Processing Units are specialized hardware accelerators designed specifically for machine learning workloads. They offer even higher performance than GPUs for certain tasks.
- FPGAs: Field-Programmable Gate Arrays are reconfigurable hardware devices that can be customized for specific applications. They can be used to accelerate specific machine learning operations or entire models.

Real-World Examples

- Tesla: Tesla uses GPUs and Kubernetes to train and deploy its self-driving car models, leveraging the parallel processing power of GPUs to handle the massive amounts of data generated by its fleet of vehicles.

- Facebook: Facebook uses GPUs and Kubernetes to power its machine learning infrastructure, including its image recognition, natural language processing, and recommendation systems.
- Google: Google uses TPUs and Kubernetes to train its large language models and power its search and advertising services.

Effectively managing and utilizing GPUs and other hardware accelerators with Kubernetes, you can significantly accelerate your machine learning workloads and achieve better performance and cost-effectiveness.

9.3 Federated Learning and Edge AI on Kubernetes

As machine learning models become more sophisticated and data becomes more distributed, we need new approaches to training and deploying these models. This is where federated learning and edge AI come in.

Think of it like a team of scientists collaborating on a research project. Each scientist has their own dataset and conducts experiments in their own lab. Instead of gathering all the data in one central location, they share their findings and collaborate to build a better model together.

Similarly, in federated learning, multiple devices or servers collaborate to train a shared model without directly sharing their data. This is particularly useful when data privacy is a concern, such as in healthcare or finance, where regulations might restrict the sharing of sensitive data.

Edge AI, on the other hand, involves deploying machine learning models directly on edge devices, such as smartphones, IoT devices, or edge servers. This allows for low-latency inference and reduces the need to transfer data to the cloud.

Federated Learning

Federated learning allows you to train machine learning models on decentralized data without moving the data to a central location. This is achieved by training local models on each device or server and then aggregating the model updates to create a global model.

Key benefits of federated learning:

- Data privacy: Preserves data privacy by keeping the data on the individual devices.
- Reduced communication costs: Avoids the need to transfer large amounts of data to the cloud.
- Improved model performance: Can lead to better model performance by leveraging diverse data sources.

How Federated Learning Works

1. Local training: Each device or server trains a local model on its own data.
2. Model updates: The devices send their model updates (e.g., gradients or weights) to a central server.
3. Aggregation: The central server aggregates the model updates to create a new global model.
4. Distribution: The updated global model is distributed back to the devices.
5. Iteration: The process repeats until the model converges.

Edge AI: Bringing Intelligence to the Edge

Edge AI involves deploying machine learning models directly on edge devices, such as smartphones, IoT devices, or edge servers. This allows for:

- Low-latency inference: Predictions can be generated quickly without the need to send data to the cloud.
- Reduced bandwidth consumption: Reduces the amount of data that needs to be transferred to the cloud.

- Offline functionality: Enables applications to function even without internet connectivity.

How Kubernetes Enables Federated Learning and Edge AI

Kubernetes provides a powerful platform for managing and orchestrating federated learning and edge AI workloads.

- **Federated learning:** Kubernetes can be used to manage the training process across multiple devices or servers, orchestrating the distribution of the global model and the aggregation of model updates.
- **Edge AI:** Kubernetes can be used to deploy and manage machine learning models on edge devices, ensuring they have the necessary resources and are running reliably.

Example: Deploying a Model to the Edge with Kubernetes

```yaml
apiVersion: v1
kind: Pod
metadata:
  name: my-edge-model
spec:
  nodeName: my-edge-node  # Schedule the pod on a specific edge node
  containers:
  - name: my-ml-container
    image: my-edge-model-image:latest
```

This configuration deploys a pod containing your edge AI model to a specific node named my-edge-node.

Tools and Frameworks for Federated Learning and Edge AI

- TensorFlow Federated: A framework for implementing federated learning with TensorFlow.
- PyTorch Mobile: A lightweight version of PyTorch for deploying models on mobile and embedded devices.
- KubeEdge: A Kubernetes-native platform for extending Kubernetes to the edge.

Real-World Examples

- Healthcare: Federated learning is used to train medical models on patient data from multiple hospitals without sharing the data between institutions.
- Finance: Federated learning is used to train fraud detection models on transaction data from multiple banks without sharing sensitive financial information.
- Autonomous vehicles: Edge AI is used to power self-driving car features, such as lane keeping and object detection, enabling real-time decision-making without relying on cloud connectivity.
- Smart home devices: Edge AI is used to enable voice recognition, facial recognition, and other intelligent features on smart home devices.

Combining the power of Kubernetes with federated learning and edge AI, you can build and deploy innovative machine learning applications that address the challenges of data privacy, latency, and bandwidth constraints.

9.4 The Evolving Landscape of Cloud-Native ML

The world of cloud-native machine learning is a dynamic and ever-evolving landscape, with new technologies, trends, and best practices emerging all the time.

Think of it like a bustling city, constantly growing and changing, with new buildings, roads, and transportation systems being developed to accommodate its expanding population and needs. Similarly, the cloud-native ML ecosystem is constantly evolving to address the growing demands of machine learning applications and the increasing complexity of data and models.

In this section, we'll explore some of the key trends and developments shaping the future of cloud-native machine learning.

1. MLOps: Streamlining the Machine Learning Lifecycle

MLOps (Machine Learning Operations) is a set of practices that aims to automate and streamline the machine learning lifecycle, from data preparation and model training to deployment and monitoring. It's like having a well-oiled machine that efficiently handles all the steps involved in building and deploying machine learning models.

Key aspects of MLOps:

- Automation: Automate repetitive tasks, such as data preprocessing, model training, and deployment.
- Collaboration: Improve collaboration between data scientists, engineers, and operations teams.
- Versioning: Track different versions of your data, code, and models.
- Monitoring: Continuously monitor the performance and health of your models in production.
- Reproducibility: Ensure that your experiments and deployments are reproducible.

Tools and platforms for MLOps:

- MLflow: An open-source platform for managing the ML lifecycle.
- Kubeflow: An open-source platform for machine learning on Kubernetes.

- Cloud AI platforms: Cloud providers offer MLOps tools and services, such as Google Cloud AI Platform and AWS SageMaker.

2. The Rise of AI Platforms

Cloud providers are investing heavily in AI platforms that provide a comprehensive suite of tools and services for building, training, and deploying machine learning models. These platforms offer:

- Pre-trained models: Access to pre-trained models for various tasks, such as image recognition and natural language processing.
- AutoML: Automated machine learning tools that can help you build and optimize models without deep expertise.
- Scalable infrastructure: Access to scalable infrastructure, such as GPUs and TPUs, for training and deploying your models.
- MLOps tools: Integrated MLOps tools for managing your machine learning lifecycle.

Examples of AI platforms:

- Google Cloud AI Platform: A comprehensive suite of tools and services for building and deploying machine learning models on Google Cloud.
- AWS SageMaker: A similar platform from Amazon Web Services.
- Azure Machine Learning: Microsoft's cloud-based machine learning platform.

3. The Power of Open Source

The open-source community is playing a crucial role in driving innovation in cloud-native machine learning. Open-source projects like Kubernetes, Kubeflow, and MLflow are providing the foundation for many machine learning platforms and tools.

Benefits of open source:

- Flexibility: You can customize and extend open-source tools to meet your specific needs.
- Cost-effectiveness: Open-source tools are often free to use.
- Community support: A large and active community can provide support and contribute to the development of open-source projects.

4. Other Trends to Watch

- Serverless machine learning: The adoption of serverless technologies like Knative for deploying machine learning models.
- Edge AI: The increasing deployment of machine learning models on edge devices.
- Explainable AI: The development of techniques to make machine learning models more transparent and explainable.
- Responsible AI: The growing focus on ethical considerations and responsible use of AI.

The field of cloud-native machine learning is constantly evolving. To stay ahead of the curve, it's important to:

- **Follow industry trends:** Keep up-to-date with the latest developments and trends in cloud-native ML.
- **Experiment with new technologies:** Explore new tools and platforms to see how they can benefit your machine learning workflows.
- **Engage with the community:** Participate in online forums, attend conferences, and contribute to open-source projects.

By embracing the evolving landscape of cloud-native machine learning, you can continue to build and deploy innovative and impactful applications that leverage the latest technologies and best practices.

Conclusion

We've reached the end of our journey through the exciting world of machine learning on Kubernetes! Throughout this book, we've explored the powerful synergy between these two transformative technologies, learning how to harness the scalability, flexibility, and efficiency of Kubernetes to build, deploy, and manage cutting-edge machine learning applications.

We started with the fundamentals, laying a solid foundation in both machine learning concepts and Kubernetes architecture. We then delved into the practical aspects of containerizing machine learning applications with Docker, orchestrating complex workflows with Argo and Kubeflow, deploying models for various use cases, and scaling our applications to meet real-world demands.

Along the way, we've emphasized the importance of security, data privacy, and best practices for managing your machine learning pipelines. We've also explored advanced topics like serverless machine learning, hardware acceleration, and the evolving landscape of cloud-native ML.

Key Takeaways

As you reflect on your journey through this book, here are some key takeaways to keep in mind:

- Kubernetes is a powerful platform for machine learning: Kubernetes provides the scalability, flexibility, and portability needed to build and deploy robust machine learning applications.
- Containerization is essential: Docker containers provide a consistent and portable environment for your machine learning applications.

- Orchestration simplifies complex workflows: Tools like Argo and Kubeflow help you manage complex machine learning pipelines.
- Security is paramount: Protect your valuable data and models by implementing robust security measures.
- Continuous learning is key: The field of cloud-native machine learning is constantly evolving. Stay informed about the latest trends and technologies.

The Future of Machine Learning on Kubernetes

The future of machine learning on Kubernetes is bright! As the adoption of both technologies continues to grow, we can expect to see even more innovation and exciting developments in this field.

Here are some trends to watch:

- Increased automation: MLOps practices will continue to mature, further automating the machine learning lifecycle.
- More sophisticated AI platforms: Cloud providers will continue to enhance their AI platforms, offering more powerful tools and services for building and deploying machine learning models.
- Greater focus on edge AI: We'll see more machine learning models deployed on edge devices, enabling new applications and use cases.
- Advancements in federated learning: Federated learning will become increasingly important for training models on decentralized data while preserving privacy.
- Ethical considerations: The ethical implications of AI will become increasingly important, and we'll see more focus on responsible AI development and deployment.

The world of machine learning on Kubernetes is full of opportunities for innovation and impact. Embrace the journey, continue to learn and experiment, and use your knowledge to build intelligent applications that can solve real-world problems and make a positive difference in the world.

Thank you for joining us on this exciting adventure! We hope this book has equipped you with the knowledge and skills you need to succeed in the world of cloud-native machine learning.

www.ingramcontent.com/pod-product-compliance
Lightning Source LLC
Chambersburg PA
CBHW082247220526
45469CB00009B/2906